Sharon Vanderlip, D

Rabbits

Everything About Selection, Care,
Nutrition, Behavior, and Training

BARRON'S

CONTENTS

INTRODUCTION TO THE RABBIT

With their endearing appearance and gentle nature, rabbits have won the hearts and captured the imaginations of millions of animal lovers worldwide. Rabbits make wonderful companions and form close bonds with their human families. It's no surprise that you have fallen under the charm of a bright-eyed bunny with beautiful, soft fur!

Rabbits need special care and handling; safe, comfortable housing; and the right kind of nutritious food. There is so much to know about rabbits! Whether you already own a rabbit or are wondering if a rabbit is the perfect pet for you, this book will give you valuable, useful, up-to-date information about the history, biology, behavior, health care, housing, reproduction, and nutritional needs of one of the world's most beloved pets—the domestic rabbit!

Role of the Rabbit

Rabbits were originally used for hunting sport, for food, and for fur. However, it didn't take long for animal lovers to discover that these engaging animals can play a much more valuable role in our lives as entertaining, educational, and affectionate companions!

Today, rabbits are the most popular exotic mammal pet in the United States and the third most popular pet after dogs and cats. You might not think of your bunny as "exotic," but rabbits differ in many ways from common domestic pet species. Rabbits have unique characteristics and special needs that differ from more common pets. In fact, when a rabbit is ill, she can be a challenging patient. In those cases, you should consult a veterinarian who has experience and expertise with rabbits whenever possible, such as a member of the Association of Exotic Mammal Veterinarians (see "Information").

Rabbits have been studied more than most animal species. As a result, we have learned how to take better care of them. In addition, many genetically pure strains of rabbits have been developed to study inherited diseases and skeletal problems in humans. We are greatly

Netherland Dwarf Himalayan Doe

indebted to rabbits used in research for their enormous role in advancing human and animal health care.

Throughout the centuries, rabbits have been introduced in many countries and islands by humans without regard for the long-term consequences. In many countries, rabbits multiplied in such astonishing numbers that they became serious "pests." They ate the vegetation, devastated the land, and led to the

Important Note

There are 24 species of rabbits. This book is about the care of the domestic pet rabbit, the descendent of the European rabbit. Throughout this book, when we refer to "rabbits," we are referring to *Oryctolagus cuniculus.*

demise of many native species. In some places, such as Australia, elaborate eradication efforts were put into place, and several million rabbits were exterminated.

Of all the many roles rabbits have played in history—food, fur, sport, research, and "pest"— our rabbits play the most important role of all, the role of companionship!

The Domestic Rabbit

Your beautiful, bright-eyed rabbit is entertaining, affectionate, inquisitive, and wonderful to touch. With good nutrition and tender loving care, your little friend may be part of your life for eight years or longer. In order to give your rabbit the best care possible, to keep her healthy, and to understand her unique personality and special needs, you should learn as much about rabbits as possible!

The European rabbit, *Oryctolagus cuniculus,* is the ancestor of all domestic rabbit breeds. Today's rabbits come in a variety of breeds, sizes, coat colors, coat textures, eye colors, ear length and carriage, and conformation. Although their appearance has changed from that of their wild ancestors, domestic rabbits still retain their special adaptations, abilities, behaviors, and instincts that have enabled the species to survive for millions of years against the harshest of odds. As animals of prey, rabbits have developed special physiological and anatomical adaptations that allow them to escape predators and to reproduce prolifically.

Rabbit Characteristics

Rabbits are animals of prey. They are easily startled. They produce sudden bursts of adrenaline to enable them to escape when startled.

Rabbit Terminology

Male rabbit	Buck
Female rabbit	Doe
Baby rabbit	Kit, bunny
Parturition (giving birth)	Kindle

Rabbits are also easily stressed. They are not able to tolerate prolonged adrenaline releases, as happens during stress.

Rabbits have numerous predators in the wild, including foxes, coyotes, cats, weasels, civets, stoats, and birds of prey. Rabbits use their keen senses to help them detect predators. A rabbit's defense mechanism is to "freeze" in position to avoid detection by predators, especially if the rabbit is exhausted, injured, or unable to run. Wild rabbits have coloration that blends in with their surroundings so they are camouflaged. If they remain still, they may go unnoticed by a predator. If detected or chased, a rabbit will try to escape danger by running, darting, dashing, and quickly changing directions to evade the pursuer until the rabbit can find refuge underground. Pet rabbits have been selectively bred so they have a wide variety of colors, patterns, markings, and body types. They are less able to hide or run from predators.

Rabbits Are Lagomorphs

Rabbits are lagomorphs (see "Rabbit Classification"). A special dental characteristic unique to lagomorphs is the presence of four upper incisors. Actually, lagomorphs are born with three pairs of upper incisors. However, the outer one on each side is small and quickly lost. The remaining incisors consist of two front upper incisors and a small pair of incisors directly behind the front pair. The second set of incisors are rounded and do not protrude much beyond the gingiva. They do not have cutting edges. They are called "peg teeth" and are found only in the upper jaw.

Skull: All lagomorphs have an elongated foreface reinforced by a latticework of bone (fenestrations). Rabbits have prominent supraoribital bones and long nasal regions.

The eyes of lagomorphs are situated high on the sides of the head and directed laterally to give the animal simultaneous binocular vision forward and backward. The large, protuberant cornea (one-third the size of the globe) has an acceptance angle of 190-degree vision. This vision partially overlaps, giving the rabbit a panoramic view to help detect predators. A small blind spot, however, is right below the mouth. So rabbits depend on their lips, whiskers, and sense of smell to find their food. Rabbits do not have a tapetum lucidum (a layer of tissue within the eye that reflects light and helps with night vision). However, they have an effective aperture under poor lighting

English Spot Lilac Doe

conditions that makes their eyes eight times more efficient than that of a human's in low light conditions. This ability sacrifices some of the rabbit's visual acuity, although rabbits are good at detecting motion. Rabbits have a third eyelid (nictitating membrane) that partially closes when they sleep. Studies of cone cells and testing indicate rabbits have some color vision to distinguish blue and green. Rabbits may not see colors the same way humans perceive them.

Ears: Rabbits have excellent hearing (360 to 42,000 Hertz). Erect rabbit ears can rotate

Tan Black

almost 270 degrees, enabling the animal to focus sound waves to detect danger. Lops are less able to focus sound waves because of their pendulous ears. Ears also serve to help dissipate heat as the ear veins dilate. Ears can also conserve body heat as the ear veins constrict. Ears make up approximately 12 percent of a rabbit's body surface area (except in breeds with small ears). Rabbit ears are always longer than they are wide.

Nose: A Y-shaped naked groove extends from the upper lip to the nose. The nose is surrounded by naked skin. This skin may be covered by surrounding fur. There is a sensory pad at the entrance to each nostril. The nostrils (nares) can be closed tightly. The internal walls of the outside of the nostrils have well developed prenarial glands of unknown function that can be exposed or hidden by voluntary movements. Because of the way the rabbit's epiglottis is positioned over the soft palate, rabbits are obligate nose breathers. This means that it is extremely difficult for them to breathe through their mouths. If a rabbit is trying to breathe through her mouth, this is a sign of very serious illness.

Mouth: Rabbit lips are sensitive and are used to help discriminate food. The only sweat glands rabbits have are confined to the lips. The incisors are separated from the mouth by thin lip folds covered with fine, velvety hair. The mouth cavity is long and narrow. It is difficult to examine without anesthesia.

Vibrissae (whiskers, stiff hairs) are important for tactile, sensory information, including food discrimination. Nose twitching helps increase tactile sensation from the vibrissae. Vibrissae are located above and below the eyes and on the face (cheeks and under the chin).

Rabbit teeth (dentition) play a very important role in rabbit health. Rabbits are lagomorphs. They have four upper incisors (front teeth) consisting of two front upper incisors and a small pair of rounded incisors (peg teeth) directly behind the front pair that do not have cutting edges.

Rabbits have 28 open rooted teeth that continue to grow throughout life. Teeth that grow throughout life are called *elodont* or *aradicular*. The portion extending above the gum line is called the clinical crown and that extending below the gum line is the reserve crown. Rabbits have long clinical crowns, referred to as hypsodont. The root of elodont teeth is more accurately called the apex.

Rabbit teeth are white and curved. A longitudinal groove is on the front surface of the incisors. Rabbits incisors, premolars, and molars (cheek teeth) continue to erupt throughout

Dental Details

Adult rabbits have 28 teeth. Their dental formula is

i = incisors	i 2/1
c = canine teeth	c 0/0
p = premolars	p 3/2
m = molars	m 3/3

The number to the left of the slash represents one-half of the upper jaw (left or right side). The number to the right of the slash represents the opposite half of the bottom jaw (left or right side). Add all the numbers and multiply by 2 to get the total number of teeth.

Many dental problems in rabbits, such as malocclusion, are hereditary.

Holland Lop Broken Tortoiseshell

life at a rate of approximately 2 to 2.4 mm per week or 4 to 5 inches (10 to 12 cm) per year.

Missing peg teeth is a trait that occurs in domestic rabbits. It is thought to be a dominant hereditary trait. The condition does not affect health or cause problems.

Extra peg teeth have also been noted in domestic rabbits. In these cases, the extra peg teeth grow between the normal peg teeth and are larger than the normal peg teeth. This trait is considered to be inherited by a single recessive gene.

Rabbits do not have canine teeth. There is a large space between the incisors and the premolars. This space is called the diastema.

Rabbits with correct dental occlusion chew with a lateral scissors-like action so that the lower incisors occlude and cut between the functional upper incisors and the peg teeth. The enamel layer in a rabbit's incisors is not evenly distributed around the tooth. More enamel is on the front of the incisor, less on the sides of the incisor, and little to no enamel is on the back of the tooth. This causes the teeth to wear in such a manner that a sharp chisel angle and cutting edge is maintained.

Rabbit Weights

Buck	4.4 to 11 lbs. (2–5 kg)
Doe	4.4 to 13.2 lbs. (2–6 kg)
Newborn kit	1 to 2.6 ounces (30–80 g)

The teeth are continually sharpened as they wear and grow. The rate of dental growth has to match the rate of tooth wear or dental problems will result.

Dewlap: Does have a large fold of skin, called a dewlap, that stretches beneath their chins and extends from ear to ear. They pull hair from their dewlaps to build nests.

Body: The thoracic (chest) cavity is small, and the heart is small. The thymus, a lymphoid gland that plays an important role in the development of the immune system, remains functional in the chest cavity throughout life. This is unlike other species, in which the thymus gland shrinks about the time of maturity.

Doe with large dewlap

A rabbit's abdomen is large compared with other species of the same size in order to accommodate its large stomach, large cecum, and extremely long intestinal tract.

Skeleton: Rabbits have a light skeleton, making up only 7 to 8 percent of the animal's body weight. (Rabbit bones are only one-third as dense as those of a cat.) Because the skeleton is delicate, rabbits often suffer fractures of the tibia or spine when not properly handled. Spinal fractures often occur at the ninth thoracic vertebra or the seventh lumbar vertebra.

Mammary gland: Does have mammary glandular tissue that extends from the throat to the groin. They have three to five pairs of nipples (teats), with an average of eight to ten teats altogether. Nipples do not develop in bucks.

Genitals: Bucks have hairless scrotal sacs. The penis is pointed and concealed within the prepuce. Does have a slit vulvar opening.

Limbs: The hind limbs are longer and markedly larger than the forelimbs. The hind limbs are designed for hopping and bounding. The main bones of the hind limb, the tibia and fibula, are fused for more than half the length of the leg.

Feet: Rabbits do not have footpads. The feet are fully haired, especially on the plantar (bottom) surface to protect the hind feet.

Toes: Five toes are on each of the front feet, but the innermost toe (hallux, "thumb") is reduced and very small. It is called a dewclaw. Four toes are on each of the hind feet.

Nails are long, straight, and sharp. All toes have nails that must be trimmed regularly, including the dewclaws.

Tail: The visible part of the tail is upturned, short, and furry.

Rabbit Facts

Origin	Spain, originally confined to the Iberian Peninsula and southern France and possibly northwest Africa at the end of the Pleistocene
Natural habitat in the wild	Savannahs, scrub, and grasslands; Living in complex burrows called warrens
Diet in the wild	Grasses, herbaceous foods, grains, may eat barks and twigs for fiber
Activity	Crepuscular: most active during dusk and dawn (taken from the French word "crépuscule" meaning twilight). Wild European rabbits can also be nocturnal, leaving burrows in the evening and returning in the early morning
Sensitivity to heat	Rabbits tolerate cold better than heat. Rabbits are very sensitive to heat. They have no sweat glands other than those on their lips. Rabbits should not be housed in areas exceeding 82.5°F (28°C).
Lifestyle	Social, gregarious, colonial
Normal body temperature (rectal)	101.3–103.5°F (38.5–39.5°C)
Illnesses	Often caused by incorrect diet, dental diseases, unsanitary housing conditions
Coat color and type	Wide variety of colors, patterns, spots, and markings; variety of coat textures
Number of chromosomes	44
Lifespan	8–11 years

Scent glands: Bucks and does have scent glands located under the chin and in the ano-genital area.

Fur: Standard breeds of rabbits have both underfur and guard hairs of variable length. The fur is characteristically dense but not durable. Angora fur is long and soft. Rex fur is deep, plush, and velvet-like.

Rabbit Measurements

Rabbit breeds vary significantly in size. Unlike most mammalian species, females are larger than males.

Special Adaptations

1. Rabbits have teeth that grow continually throughout life.

2. Rabbits have long, powerful hind limbs adapted for quick movement and designed for leaping and bounding to escape predators.

3. Rabbits have a large cecum (about ten times the size of the rabbit's small stomach) and a very long intestinal tract to allow for better digestion.

4. Rabbits use hind gut fermentation and digestion. Most digestion takes place in the large intestine and cecum (see "Feeding Your Rabbit").

5. It is natural for a rabbit to eat soft feces passed during the evening. This is called coprophagy, or cecotrophy. Cecotropes (also known as night feces or soft feces) differ from the dry, normal hard fecal pellets passed during the day. Cecotropes are soft fecal pellets encased in mucus in small bunches. They have a light green sheen and contain protein, B complex vitamins, dietary minerals, and crude fiber. Rabbits eat cecotropes directly from the anus in the early morning hours. Cecotrope consumption is a part of normal circadian behavior and is necessary for the rabbit to extract valuable nutrients. Bunnies begin eating their mother's cecotropes at two weeks of age and their own cecotropes at about three weeks of age (see "Feeding Your Rabbit").

The Rabbit's Place in Natural History

Rabbits have been around for a very long time. Identifiable rabbit fossils date back to the Oligocene (about 30 million years ago). The oldest European rabbit fossil found to date is 6½ million years old.

Rabbit Classification

All living creatures—animals, plants, and insects—are classified and grouped according to their similarities and differences. Names are assigned according to kingdom, phylum, class, order, family, genus, and species. With each progressive category, animals grouped together are more closely related.

Rabbit taxonomy has been one of the most controversial topics in mammalian classification since the system of species classification was first established by Carolus Linnaeus (also known as Karl von Linne or Carl von Linné) in the 18th century. Rabbits and rodents share many similarities. In 1758, Linnaeus classified them together in a group called Glires. This group was later classified as the order Rodentia and divided into two suborders: Simplicidentata (animals with one pair of upper incisors) and Duplicidentata (animals with a second set of upper incisors placed directly behind the first set). The suborder Duplicidentata encompassed pikas, hares, and rabbits. In 1912, the

Mini Rex Tri

Rabbit Taxonomy for the Domestic *Oryctolagus cuniculus*

Kingdom *Animalia* (animal kingdom)

Phylum *Chordata* (animals having spinal columns)

Subphylum *Vertebrata* (vertebrates)

Class *Mammalia* (mammals: animals that nourish their young with milk from mammary glands)

Infraclass *Eutheria* (placental mammals)

Infraclass *Glires* (Lagomorpha and Rodentia)

Order *Lagomorpha* (two families: *Leporidae*—rabbits and hares; and *Ochotonidae*—pikas)

Family *Leporidae* (rabbits and hares)

Genus *Oryctolagus*: (one species: the European rabbit *cuniculus*)

Mini Satin Red

Duplicidentata became the order Lagomorpha and was recognized as being distinct from Rodentia. Since that time, scientists have continued to debate the evolutionary relationship of lagomorphs and rodents. Some researchers suggested that rabbits share some skeletal similarities with Artiodactyla (an order that includes a wide variety of animals with hooves, such as pigs, camels, and goats).

Rabbit taxonomy may return full circle to Glires. We have gained additional information from molecular studies, DNA analysis, and comparisons among species. We have also gained valuable information from recent fossil findings. In particular, a tiny extinct rodent from the late Paleocene found in Inner Mongolia, China, called *Tribosphenomys minutus*, has provided much information. Together, these data suggest that rabbits and rodents

American Blue

may indeed be more closely related than previously thought. If that proves correct, the word Glires may again be used to encompass lagomorphs and rodents.

Rabbit Relatives

Pikas (genus *Ochotonidae*) are lagomorphs. However, they have a long-distinct ancestry from Leporidae since at least the Eocene (50 million years ago) and look much different from their rabbit and hare relatives. Pikas are also known as mouse hares or coneys. There are more than 20 living species of pikas (reports vary from 22 to 25). Pikas average 8 inches (200 mm) or less in length and weigh less than 1 pound (100–400 g). They have short blunt heads, short rounded ears, and no visible tail. They have fewer teeth than rabbits as they

Differences Between Rabbits and Hares

Rabbits	Hares
24 species	23 species
Chromosomes (diploid number) 44	Chromosomes (diploid number) 48
Ears vary in size and carriage, may be erect or pendulous (lops)	Larger ears than rabbits, black tipped, and with distinguishing skull features
In the wild, digs and lives in complex underground burrows or warrens with multiple entrances that they plug or open as needed; Highly territorial	Nonburrowing
Gestation period 29–35 days	Gestation period up to 50 days
Build elaborate nests to kindle (give birth)	Do not build nests; Kindle in open depressions in the ground
Babies are born naked, with eyes and ears shut	Born fully furred with eyes and ears open and able to run
Requires mother's care for two to three weeks	Precocious young do not need prolonged maternal care
Social, gregarious, live in communities	Solitary
Easy to raise in captivity	Not easy to raise in captivity
Historically limited to the Iberian Peninsula and Mediterranean region	Expansive natural distribution
More evolutionarily diverse than hares (or pikas)	

Mini Rex Broken Black

have only four upper molars total, compared with six in a rabbit.

Rabbit Species

There are 10 genera of rabbits, totaling 24 rabbit species. Only one species of rabbit is in the genus *Oryctolagus*. It is the species *cuniculus*. Your pet rabbit is *Oryctolagus cuniculus* and is a direct descendent of the European rabbit.

Rabbits and Hares Do Not Interbreed!

Rabbits and hares both belong to the family Leporidae, but they do not interbreed.

When domestic rabbits (*Oryctolagus cuniculus*) are experimentally inseminated with sperm from the snowshoe hare (*Lepus americanus*), European hare (*Lepus europaeus*), or cottontail rabbit (*Sylvilagus transitionalis*), some eggs become fertilized. However, the embryos die in early development. When sperm from the domestic rabbit (*Oryctolagus cuniculus*) is used to inseminate hares, fertilization rarely occurs.

Splitting Hares!

Belgian hares, Rock hares, and Hispid hares are not hares. They are rabbits!

Jack rabbits and snow rabbits are not rabbits. They are hares!

History

The precise origins of today's domestic rabbit are still not entirely clear. However, archaeology and DNA research have brought us closer to unraveling our rabbit's mysterious history. Studies indicate that the Leporidae ancestors of today's rabbits and hares were first present in America and Asia, and that during the early

Himalayan Lilac

Tertiary, they eventually migrated from Asia to Europe. By the end of the Pleistocene, they were present in Europe.

Silver Fox

The Phoenicians are credited as being the first to discover rabbits during their voyages to the African coasts and Iberian Peninsula around 1100 B.C. Since earliest recorded history, Spain has been considered the original home of the European rabbit, *Oryctolagus cuniculus.* This theory is supported by archaeological evidence and DNA tests. The oldest-known rabbit fossil was discovered in Andalusia and dates back 6½ million years. Studies of mitochondrial DNA have confirmed the existence of two separate maternal lineages of the European rabbit, which scientists call lineage A and lineage B for simplicity. These DNA tests support the theory of northern Spain and possibly southern France as having been areas of refuge for rabbit populations during glaciation.

They also suggest that diversification within each lineage occurred independently about 2 million years ago. Finally, mitochondrial DNA studies indicate that rabbits living on the Tunisian island of Zembra are the offspring of rabbits introduced to the island at least 2,000 years ago.

Ancient writings: Interestingly, the writings of Polybios (Greek historian, ca. 200–118 B.C., also known as Polybius) and Pliny the Elder (Roman author, naturalist, philosopher, A.D. 23–79) support the assumption that European rabbits were already present on the Tyrrhenean islands during their time. Polybios is said to have seen rabbits coming from Corsica and called them "the most graceful cuniculi." This may be, in part, how the European rabbit acquired its species name *cuniculus*. However, scientists now believe that these ancient authors had confused *Oryctolagus cuniculus* with a different lagomorph species, *Prolagus sardus*. Although *Prolagus sardus* is now extinct, it was abundant in Corsica and Sardinia during the time of these authors. Excavations and research indicate *Oryctolagus cuniculus* was actually absent from the Tyrrhenean islands during Polybios and Pliny's time!

What does all of this mean? It means we have learned a lot about our pets' ancient past, but we still have much to learn! Rabbits are complicated creatures and masters at confusing and surprising us. As we continue to gain new information, we may have to change some of the ways we think about our pets. We may need to update some sections of our rabbit history books, too.

Romans: Historians report that in the first century, Romans kept rabbits enclosed in plastered high-walled gardens called *leporaria*. Some were released for hunting purposes, and many established wild populations. In the Middle Ages, this concept was expanded to enclosing large areas of land, often many acres. These medieval warrens remained popular for centuries for keeping rabbits available for hunting and food.

Population expansion: Between the 9th and 16th centuries, wild rabbit populations continued to expand throughout western Europe. Rabbits were transported on long oceanic voyages and released on hundreds of islands for the purpose of reproducing and serving as a food source. They often multiplied in astounding numbers and caused much devastation.

Domestication and breeding: In the 16th century, rabbit breeding and true domestication of the species began in European (especially French) monasteries. With selective breeding and domestication, rabbits diversified in size, body shape, ear length, coat color, and type in a relatively short time period. By 1700, seven mutant color types were already identified. Between 1700 and 1850, two additional mutations for coat color and the factor causing angora hair were known.

Netherland Dwarf Tan

Mini Lop Broken Checkered

Rabbit breeding became a popular hobby in America at the end of the 19th century, and a large number of pet rabbits were imported

to the United States from Europe during that time. One of the catalysts for this was what was referred to as the "Belgian Hare Boom." The Belgian hare is actually a rabbit. The breed was developed to resemble true hares, with a racy, refined body and red color. A few animals were imported by a Mr. E. M. Hughes. They reached New York in 1888 and became a sensation. E. M. Hughes, together with W. N. Richardson and G. W. Felton, founded the first rabbit club in America, the American Belgian Hare Association. During the "Belgian Hare Boom," from 1898 to 1901, thousands of Belgian hares were imported to America. They were purchased by some of the wealthiest entrepreneurs of the time for astronomical prices. (Ironically, by the 1940s, the Belgian hare had become a rare breed.) As more breeds of rabbits were imported and the United States rabbit population grew, so did the number of rabbit enthusiasts and breeders. In 1910, the American Rabbit Breeders Association (ARBA) was formed.

The ARBA states that it "is an organization dedicated to the promotion, development and improvement of the domestic rabbit and cavy" (guinea pig). The ARBA currently recognizes 47 rabbit breeds. For each breed, there is a long story about the breed's history and the people who raised, promoted, and maintained the breed to make it what it is today. Detailed information on the history and introduction of individual breeds and varieties can be obtained directly from the specific breed clubs, the ARBA, and an excellent book by Bob Whitman called *Domestic Rabbits and Their Histories: Breeds of the World* (see "Information").

Variety: Rabbits are remarkably diverse. There seems to be no limit to the variations in

Spotted Rabbit

color, type, conformation, and size that can be created with careful selective breeding. So what about those two original maternal lines from which all living European rabbits have descended? It's hard to believe, but mitochondrial DNA studies show that all of today's domestic breeds descend from only one of those two lines—line B! This means that it is possible that as early as the 11th century, most of the rabbits that were starting to spread throughout Europe were likely the descendents of line B.

With all of our domestic rabbits tracing back to a single maternal line, how can they all be so different? That is one of the many rabbit mysteries that scientists are trying to figure out. Clearly, our remarkable rabbit friends still have a lot to teach us!

Lagomorph Legend and Lore

Rabbits are a big part of our lives and our culture. As children, we have known and grown to love them in stories, books, films, and television. Here are just a few. See how many more you can add to the list!

- *The Velveteen Rabbit*
- Peter Cottontail
- Peter Rabbit
- *Pat the Bunny*
- Benjamin Bunny
- Rabbit in *Winnie-The-Pooh*
- Hazel and Fiver in *Watership Down*
- The Country Bunny
- *The Runaway Bunny*
- The Easter Bunny
- Thumper in Bambi
- Bugs Bunny
- Br'er Rabbit
- The White Rabbit and March Hare in *Alice's Adventures in Wonderland*
- The Hare in *The Tortoise and the Hare*
- *Crusader Rabbit*
- Roger Rabbit
- *Harvey*
- The Trix rabbit, the Energizer Bunny, and the Duracell Bunny in commercials

BEFORE YOU BUY

If you are looking for a pet that is affectionate, beautiful, entertaining, small, quiet, clean, wonderful to pet, and has a unique personality all its own—then a rabbit just might be the perfect pet for you! Rabbits are not difficult to care for, but they do have special requirements. Learn as much as you can about rabbits before adding one to your family!

Special Considerations

Rabbits differ from more common pets in many ways. They need owners who understand them, recognize their needs, and know how to take good care of them. The most important consideration when you are thinking about bringing a rabbit into your life is you. What is your lifestyle like? Will you have time for a rabbit—not just now, but for the next eight to eleven years, maybe longer? Will a rabbit fit in with your work schedule, travel plans, and family activities? Can you offer a deserving bunny a safe and loving home? You will surely have to make some changes to your home and lifestyle to accommodate the newcomer. Are you willing to make a long-term commitment to your new rabbit and do whatever is necessary to keep your new friend safe and healthy?

Adding a new rabbit to your home and life should be a happy, positive experience for both you and your pet! The kind of companion your rabbit turns out to be depends on the kind of owner you are. If you give your rabbit lots of love and attention and the best of care, your pet will reward you with many happy years of friendship, fun, and affection.

It is well documented that people who own pets gain many psychological and physiological benefits from the human-animal bond they form. Pet owners feel needed and loved because their animals depend on them for food and care. Pets give companionship in return. Medical research suggests that people who own pets may live longer than people who do not. Studies also show that caressing an animal causes the brain to release oxytocin, a hormone that plays an important role in emotions like maternal bonding, trust, desire for social connection, and stress reduction. So if you think you are happier and feel better after petting a bunny, you are right!

Sadly, some people (such as those with allergies or with compromised immune systems) simply cannot have animals in their lives, no matter

how much they love animals. It is possible to develop allergies to rabbit hair, dander, urine, and some kinds of cage bedding material. If you tend to develop allergies, discuss them with your physician before acquiring any new pet.

Age and Longevity

A rabbit's lifespan varies, depending on the care and nutrition she receives, her breed, and her genetics. With excellent care, rabbits can live more than ten years. Rabbit ownership is a very long-term commitment.

Your Expectations

The kind of bunny you bring into your life depends on your expectations and your long-range plans for your new pet. Are you simply seeking a gentle, affectionate friend? Are you also considering exhibiting at rabbit shows? Do you think you might want to raise rabbits? You may already have an idea of the color,

size, age, and sex of the rabbit you are seeking. Perhaps you already have a particular breed in mind. Instead, you might be completely open-minded about welcoming the right rabbit when you find it, with no preconceived notions about what it will be like.

What is your schedule like? Rabbits are crepuscular creatures. They are happy to visit during the daylight hours, but they also enjoy napping during the day. If you enjoy the twilight hours yourself, it's a great time for you and your rabbit to spend more time together.

Keep your expectations reasonable and realistic. Don't expect your new rabbit to be similar to common pets or to be exactly like a previous rabbit you may have once loved in the past. Keep your mind and your heart open. When you find your perfect match, simply let her surprise you with her own unique behaviors and personality. You won't be disappointed—you'll be enchanted!

The Right Timing

Every rabbit deserves a loving home and the best of care—for her entire life! If you are already convinced that a rabbit is the perfect pet for you, make sure the timing is perfect, too. If you have several obligations and your free time is limited, or if you are changing jobs, moving, getting married, returning to school, or going on vacation, then postpone your rabbit search until you have more time to enjoy your new pet.

Animal shelters: Thousands of rabbits are abandoned at animal shelters every year, often the victims of impulse buyers or holiday shoppers. Impulse buyers purchase pets on the spur of the moment, without first learning about the species, the kind of care rabbits require, or whether the rabbit is a suitable pet for them. Impulse buyers often relinquish their pets when they realize their expectations for their pets were unreasonable, or the animals required more time and care than they anticipated, or live longer than they thought they would.

Holiday shoppers looking for rabbits are usually the worst around Easter, when many people buy bunnies as gifts for children. During the rabbit's long life span, young children can lose interest in the animal. Older children grow up and leave home, leaving the rabbit behind with the parents. Some of the most common reasons people use for relinquishing their rabbits at the animal shelters are "the children are no longer interested in the animal," "not enough time," or "didn't know the rabbit would live so long when we bought it."

Some people give up their rabbits for other reasons, such as moving or allergies. As the reasons add up, so do the numbers of homeless rabbits. Countless rabbits are in animal shelters and rabbit rescue organizations. All of them need and deserve loving homes.

Into the wild: Worse than abandoning a rabbit at an animal shelter is releasing one into the wild. A pet rabbit should never be released in the outdoors where she can fall prey to predators or neighborhood dogs, die from heatstroke or starvation, or be run over by a vehicle.

Rabbit rescue organizations and animal shelters do their best to place homeless rabbits. However, if people made wise decisions from the onset and acted responsibly, the need for rescues and shelters would be reduced.

Think it through: Don't buy a rabbit for someone else as a gift or a surprise. People want to choose their own bunnies to make sure the animals have the personalities and characteristics they want. Rabbit ownership and care is a responsibility that each person has to assume individually.

If you are thinking of acquiring a rabbit for the children in your family, do not hold the children responsible for the care of the rabbit. Children can help take care of a rabbit, but adults are ultimately responsible. If you brought the rabbit into the family, then you are the person responsible for the rabbit throughout her entire life!

Cost

Rabbit prices vary according to the kind of rabbit (mixed or pure breed, show or pet rabbit, and genetics/pedigree), age, sex, and even color and markings.

The greatest expense of rabbit ownership is not the purchase price of the animal. It encompasses all the costs involved in time, housing, bedding, food, space, accessories, and, when needed, veterinary care.

Time

Rabbits are not demanding pets, but they do require time for interactions and play and exploration time. The following care items must be performed daily to ensure that your bright-eyed, beautiful bunny is healthy and happy!

1. Give fresh food and water.

2. Check the water level in the bottle. Make sure the sipper tube is working properly and that it is not plugged.

3. Empty and clean the litter box.

4. Pet and visit with your rabbit. Make sure she is healthy and eating, drinking, urinating, defecating, and behaving normally.

Materials

Rabbits require some basic essentials:

✔ Safe, comfortable, escape-proof housing
✔ Nutritious food (hay and pellets)
✔ A litter box
✔ A comfortable platform or washable rug to sit on to rest their feet so their feet don't get sore on hard surfaces
✔ Safe, absorbent bedding material
✔ Hanging water bottle with metal sipper tube
✔ Heavy, nonspill ceramic crocks
✔ Hanging feeder
✔ Hay rack
✔ Hideaways
✔ Toys for chewing, nudging, and tossing

Space

Today, more rabbits than ever live indoors as house pets. House rabbits have interesting lives. They get to spend lots of time watching home activities and interacting with the family. They are also healthier than outdoor rabbits because they are not subjected to the stresses of outdoor living, such as predators, disease exposure, parasites (flies, mosquitoes, ticks), and harsh weather (especially heat).

Your rabbit needs space to be active, stretch out, lie down, sit up, hop about, and explore. Not so long ago, many people thought it was fine simply to put a rabbit into a small cage and leave her there with nothing to do but eat and nap until someone found the time to take her out and play with her. What a sad and boring existence that was for a bunny. Fortunately, that mentality has changed. Rabbit enthusiasts recognize that rabbits are inquisitive, playful creatures that need space to play and explore, as well as a place to hide and sleep—and that indoor living is more enjoy-

Essentials of Rabbit Care

✔ Nutritious, balanced diet and fresh water
✔ Space to run, play, explore
✔ Safe places to hide and sleep
✔ Clean, dry housing
✔ Litter box with safe, clean bedding material
✔ Comfortable temperature and humidity
✔ Interesting toys and activities for social enrichment
✔ Regular grooming
✔ Lots of love and attention from you

able for the rabbit and her owner! A mentally stimulated rabbit is a much more interesting and entertaining pet, too.

In addition to a safe, sufficiently large habitat for your rabbit, plan on setting up a protected, bunny-proofed space where your rabbit can play and investigate. These areas may include a hallway in the house, an enclosed area in an extra bedroom, or space in the yard or patio sheltered from sun and predatory animals (see "Accommodations for Your Rabbit").

Rabbits and Other Pets

Rabbits are gregarious, social animals. In the wild, they live together in colonies. You don't need a colony to keep your furry friend happy, but your rabbit would not enjoy solitude. Rabbits thrive on the companionship of other rabbits. Because rabbits are so sociable, many rabbit adoption groups will not place a rabbit into a single-rabbit family home. Rabbits bond closely with each other, sometimes taking a while to bond. If you have two rabbits that are bonded with each other, don't worry. They will still bond with you, too!

Rabbits housed together: Rabbits housed together must be neutered to reduce quarreling, dominance behavior, and other unwanted behavior and to prevent reproduction. You can pair two females together, or one male and one female together. Males should not be housed together because they can be aggressive toward one another, even if neutered. Rabbits don't bond immediately. They need time to get to know each other. Make introductions in a safe, supervised environment. It can take several days to several weeks before some rabbits accept each other. After they have bonded though, they remain friends and enjoy each other's companionship. (see "Understanding Your Rabbit" for bonding methods).

Other pets: Rabbits have a very keen sense of smell, so they know when other animals are in the home. Some rabbits are stressed by the scent of potential predators (cats and dogs). However, well-socialized rabbits can and do bond with friendly, gentle cats and dogs. Not all breeds of dogs are safe to introduce to your rabbit. Some hunting dogs cannot suppress their natural instincts and would consider your bunny to be fabulous quarry. Your rabbit would sense the danger and be terrified and extremely stressed. Every

Use Caution!

To prevent accidental injury, always make sure the doors to your rabbit's enclosure are securely fastened and out of reach of the family pets. Never leave your pets alone together, no matter how compatible they seem to be.

animal is different, so be careful. Your rabbit may or may not be compatible with your other pets. If you decide to introduce your rabbit to them, do so cautiously, only one animal at a time. Always be sure your rabbit is not frightened, and supervise your pets to make sure your rabbit cannot be harmed. Remember that a cat's toenails are formidable weapons that can inflict serious injury, especially to a rabbit's eyes. Play it safe! Keep your cat's toenails trimmed! You can also use plastic nail covers designed for cat claws, available at pet stores.

Rabbits and guinea pigs (cavies) are compatible, and you will often see them housed together. Although this is all right for a rabbit, it is not the best situation for a guinea pig. Guinea pigs can contract *Bordetella bronchiseptica* from some rabbits. This bacteria causes severe respiratory disease in guinea pigs. If you are thinking of housing rabbits and guinea pigs together, ask your veterinarian about vaccinating your guinea pigs against bronchiseptica for added protection.

Selecting a Veterinarian

Rabbits do very well with loving care and good nutrition. However, if your furry friend is sick or injured, she will need veterinary care immediately. The sooner your pet is diagnosed and treated, the better her chances are for recovery.

Some veterinarians specialize in exotic mammals or have a special interest in them. Rabbits have nutritional and health care needs different from common companion animals and can be very sensitive to medications used for treating more common pets.

Select a veterinarian *before* you purchase your rabbit and *before* your pet needs health care. That way, you won't lose precious time trying to find a veterinarian during a possible emergency situation.

You and your veterinarian will work together to keep your rabbit healthy throughout her life. Be as particular about choosing a veterinarian as you are about selecting your own doctor.

Interest and expertise: Find a veterinarian who appreciates rabbits as much as you do and who has expertise in treating them. Ask rabbit breeders, rabbit clubs, and rabbit rescue organizations which veterinarians they recommend. Personal recommendations are among the best ways to find a good veterinarian. Both the Association of Exotic Mammal Veterinarians and the American Veterinary Medical Association can give you a list of veterinarians in your area who have rabbit experience and expertise (see "Information").

Priorities
No matter what kind of rabbit you are looking for, health and temperament should always be your first priorities when choosing a bunny.

Consider hours and location: Ideally, you should be able to drive to the veterinarian's office within a reasonable amount of time. The practice should be open 24 hours for emergencies.

Choosing Your Rabbit

You can find rabbits in many places, such as rabbit breeders, rabbit rescue organizations, animal shelters, and pet stores. If you are simply looking for a great pet and if color, breed, sex, and age do not matter much, you will have plenty of options. However, if you are seeking something very specific, it may take longer to find your ideal bunny.

Rabbit rescues and animal shelters: There are many rabbits in need of homes to be found at rabbit rescues and animal shelters. They may be mixed breeds or pure breeds, different ages and sizes, and various colors and coat types. These animals will also vary in the amount of socialization they have received as well as their friendliness, depending on their past experiences. If you are thinking about adopting a rabbit from one of these sources, be sure to talk with the placement counselors to learn more about the rabbit and if she has any special needs, so you can determine if she is the right match for you.

Pet stores: You can also find rabbits in pet stores. Be sure to talk to the store manager to learn more about the rabbit's background. Obtain as much information about the animal as you can. Ask to hold and pet the rabbit so you can see how she responds to you.

Breeders: If your heart is set on a specific breed, then you will first have to find a reputable, responsible rabbit breeder. An excellent source for rabbit breeders is the American Rabbit Breeders Association (ARBA). The ARBA can also put you in contact with breed clubs (see "Information"). You may also find rabbits through organizations such as 4-H and by attending rabbit shows at fairs and agricultural events. You can find breeders through pet magazines such as *Rabbits USA* and *Critters USA* (see "Information"). Your veterinarian may also be able to recommend breeders to you.

If you purchase from a breeder, you may have the opportunity to see the animals and visit the rabbitry (rabbit-housing facilities), ask the breeder questions, and possibly have a greater selection from which to choose. The breeder can give you information about the rabbit's temperament, age, health, diet, housing, parents, genetic background, health guarantees, and sales contracts. The breeder can also recommend a veterinarian experienced in treating rabbits. Be prepared to wait for the right rabbit. The breed, sex, color, age, and personality you want may not be immediately available.

How to Choose Your Rabbit

Select your rabbit very carefully! Use your head first and then your heart! You are choosing a friend that will be with you for many years. You want to be sure that you and your rabbit are a perfect match.

Take your time: You might be tempted to take home the first bunny you find. It is wiser to take your time and look at as many animals as you can before making a selection. This way you can compare the different animals' overall health, personalities, and sociability; the cleanliness of their environments; breeds and mixed breeds; color varieties; health guarantees; and prices.

Health and temperament: Your rabbit's health and temperament are the most important selection criteria. Every animal is different. Take your time. Carefully interact with, handle, and examine each rabbit you are considering. After you have selected a rabbit that appeals to you, take extra time to hold and interact with her to see how she behaves and responds to you.

Important! *The breeder, rabbit rescue, or animal shelter will ask you lots of questions, too, to make sure you can provide a good home for a rabbit!*

Quick Rabbit Health Check
✔ Normal weight, body in good condition, not thin, and not overweight
✔ Behaving normally
✔ Eating, drinking, urinating, and defecating normally
✔ Eyes bright, clear, and free of discharge
✔ Incisors correctly aligned in mouth, no malocclusion
✔ Ears and nose clean and free of discharge
✔ Ears and skin free of parasites, sores, crusts, and scabs
✔ Anal and genital areas clean, no signs of discharge or diarrhea
✔ Feet clean (top and bottom), no nasal discharge present on top of front feet, no foot sores, no overgrown nails
✔ Beautiful coat condition

Male or female? Both male and female rabbits make wonderful companions. Whether you have a buck or a doe, your rabbit should be neutered or spayed. This will prevent cancer or other diseases and infections of the reproductive organs. Spaying or neutering also helps prevent unwanted behavior such as aggressive territorial behavior, mounting, and urine spraying. When choosing, remember the following.

• Females are usually larger than males.
• Females tend to have more reproductive health problems (including cancer and infections) than males, so they must be spayed if they are not used for breeding.
• An adult female rabbit that was recently housed with a male may be pregnant.

Age: Bunnies should not be taken from their mothers and placed into homes before eight weeks of age. They should be eating solid food and completely weaned before they leave their mother. Bunnies are more active than adults, are more inquisitive, and seem to have a way of getting into mischief. You will have to supervise your bunny closely and socialize her. You may be able to train her to use a litter box. As your bunny grows, you will adjust how much you feed her according to her changing nutritional needs.

Adolescent and adult rabbits should be neutered. They are usually calmer and easier to train than bunnies.

How Many Rabbits to Keep?

The number of rabbits you keep depends on how much time, space, and money you have to dedicate to them. If you want to raise rabbits, you will obviously need at least one pair to begin your project (see "Raising Rabbits"). You will also have to be very sure that you have

Twelve Questions to Ask About Your Bunny

1. Is the rabbit healthy? Has she been examined by a veterinarian?
2. What kind of personality/temperament does she have?
3. How old is the rabbit?
4. What sex is it? Is it neutered (castrated) or spayed (ovariohysterovaginectomy)?
5. What kind of food does the rabbit eat and how much does she eat every day?
6. What kind of housing does she have?
7. Is there a health guarantee?
8. If the rabbit is purebred, it she registered with the American Rabbit Breeders Association and are the registration certificate and pedigree available?
9. Will the breeder/seller be available to answer questions in the future?
10. If, for some reason, you can no longer keep your rabbit, is the breeder willing to take her back or help you place your pet in a new home?
11. Can you visit the breeder's rabbitry and the rabbit's parents?
12. Can the breeder recommend a veterinarian with rabbit expertise?

loving, permanent homes lined up for your bunnies before you even allow your rabbits to breed. Too many homeless rabbits are in rescues and shelters. You don't want to contribute to the problem!

Keep only a pair of rabbits at first. This will allow you to learn as much as possible about them and help you decide if you really want to become involved in such a major undertaking as rabbit breeding.

Keep your rabbit numbers reasonable so most of the time you spend with your pets is fun time rather than clean-up time. Keep in mind the following.

• Rabbits are naturally very social animals.
• Consider keeping two rabbits so they can bond and keep each other company.
• Unless you are raising rabbits, have your pets neutered or spayed.

Children and Rabbits

Rabbits can make wonderful pets for children. However, *adults should always supervise children who are interacting with any animal.* Every rabbit has a unique personality. Some are friendlier than others; some enjoy being petted or held more than others. How a rabbit interacts and responds to a child depends on the animal's amount of socialization, personality, age, breed, health, and a myriad of other factors. It also depends on the child.

Children vary in age and maturity. Rabbits are not ideal pets for very young children because small children have difficulty safely lifting and holding rabbits. A child can accidentally drop a rabbit and injure the animal or be badly scratched by her sharp nails. It is safer for small children to observe the rabbit in her enclosure or pet her while an adult holds the pet. Children must learn not to grasp or grab at the rabbit and not to make loud noises that can frighten the animal.

Rabbits make interesting and educational pets for older, mature children who can learn the proper way to handle a rabbit (see "HOW-TO: Handling Your Rabbit"). Older children can be taught how to be kind, gentle, careful, and responsible. Many children in

groups such as 4-H are quite successful in rabbit handling and exhibiting skills. They also love their rabbits!

Children can learn a lot from a rabbit, including the importance of humane treatment and good care. They can learn to help and participate in a rabbit's daily care. Of course, rabbit ownership is a long-term commitment. As the parent, the rabbit's care will always be your responsibility.

Your Favorite Rabbit

Choose your rabbit according to her health, personality, and physical attributes and also your personal preferences. Of all the rabbits you handle and hold, the healthiest and friendliest will surely be the one to weave her way into your heart. The hardest thing about choosing a rabbit—or two—is leaving the other rabbits behind!

UNDERSTANDING YOUR RABBIT

Your rabbit's instincts, senses, behavior, communication, and body language reflect those of her wild ancestors and are integrally linked to survival. The better you understand your rabbit and her behaviors, the greater compassion you will feel for her, the more you will appreciate her, the closer you both will bond, and the more you will enjoy each other's company!

The Basics

Rabbit behavior is intimately linked to survival. As animals of prey, rabbits developed a variety of natural behaviors to help them survive predation. A domestic pet rabbit's behavior may be modified somewhat, depending on the animal and the circumstances. However, certain aspects of rabbit behavior are so deeply and genetically engrained that they are difficult, if not impossible, to change.

Rabbits have special adaptations to help them survive predation. These include keen hearing, panoramic vision to help detect predators, and powerful hind limbs to allow them to escape danger.

Rabbits can vary as much in behavior and personality as their owners can vary. Some rabbits are more friendly than others, some are outgoing, others are timid. Much of a rabbit's behavior is instinctive, and some is breed related. A rabbit's behavior is greatly influenced by the way she was raised from the time she was very young, imprinting, past experiences, and the kind of handling and attention the animal has received throughout her life.

Understanding basic bunny behavior, communication, and adaptations can help you provide a pleasant, comfortable, safe environment for your pet. It can also help prevent possible problems or stressful situations for both of you and make life together much more enjoyable!

Rabbits rely on their keen senses for information about their environment. They respond and behave accordingly. For example, the following instinctive behaviors help a rabbit survive and escape danger.

1. Remain motionless in place (freeze) to blend in with the surroundings and to avoid being detected.

2. Hide in a sheltered or covered place whenever there is danger.

3. Flee, by darting, dashing, leaping, bounding, and suddenly changing directions.

4. Find refuge underground as soon as possible.

5. Lunge and bite aggressively when threatened, frightened, or cornered.

We can use our knowledge and understanding about our pets' natural behavior to enhance and enrich their environments and make them feel safe and secure.

Your Rabbit's Five Senses

Just like humans, rabbits have five senses that allow them to learn about their environment.

Sense of sight (vision): Rabbit eyes are adapted to give them the maximum advantage in detecting predators. Rabbits have a wide, panoramic field of vision due to their prominent eyes, the lateral placement of the eyes on the head, and their small binocular field of vision to the rear. When a rabbit raises her head to be on the lookout, her range of vision widens even more. Rabbits have good night vision. Studies indicate that rabbits can distinguish blue and green colors.

Sense of hearing (auditory): Rabbits have excellent hearing, ranging from 360 to 42,000 Hz. (Human hearing ranges from 64 to 23,000 Hz.) Erect rabbit ears can rotate almost 270 degrees. This lets the animal focus sound waves to each ear individually, listening in different directions at the same time, in order to detect danger. Note that lops are not able to hear as well as rabbits with erect ears because lops have pendulous ears. Some lops may also have narrower ear canals than other rabbit breeds.

Sense of smell (olfactory): Rabbits have a very keen sense of smell. Sense of smell is very important for rabbits. It allows them to find food, explore their surroundings, detect predators, identify other animals, and find mates. Rabbits have about 100 million olfactory sensory neurons (receptor cells), compared with 5 or 6 million in a human.

Sense of taste: Rabbits can be very fussy about what they like to eat. Taste discrimination plays a large role in a rabbit's food preferences. Taste and smell are closely related. Rabbits have a very keen sense of taste, due in large part to their sensitive taste buds. Rabbit taste buds have a complicated structure and are located in the numerous foliate papillae at

Healthy rabbits groom themselves frequently throughout the day.

the sides of the base of the tongue. Each papillae resembles a tiny, cone-shaped bump or protuberance on the tongue. In each individual papillae are approximately 7,000 taste buds!

Sense of touch (tactile): Vibrissae (whiskers, stiff hairs) are important for receiving tactile, sensory information, including food discrimination. Nose twitching helps increase tactile sensation from the vibrissae. Vibrissae are located above and below the eyes and on the face (cheeks and under the chin). They also help rabbits navigate in the dark (or in underground warrens).

Behavior and Body Language

Rabbits are very expressive, sensitive animals. You will easily recognize the times your rabbit feels comfortable and secure by her behavior, posture, and body language and also by the sounds (vocalizations) she makes.

Wild rabbits live together in highly complex social groups in warrens. Does in the warrens are usually related. Dominant bucks are territorial and drive younger males out of the warren. This wild behavior is retained in domestic rabbits. Compatible rabbits enjoy snuggling together and grooming one another (females together or a single male together with females). However, bucks will fight with each other and can seriously injure or kill one another.

Keeping a rabbit isolated in a cage without companionship or environmental enrichment is not only quite different from a rabbit's natural gregarious colony lifestyle but is cruel. Like any other animal that is confined in a small space with no friends to visit and nothing to do, rabbits become bored, can become fearful, and can develop behavior problems. A bunny raised alone in isolation cannot learn how to interact appropriately with humans or with members of her own species. When introduced to humans, she may be frightened or unfriendly. When introduced to other rabbits, she may be aggressive, shy, or fearful. In these cases, rabbits can take a long time to bond with people or learn to coexist peacefully with other rabbits.

Sleep habits: Rabbits are creatures of the twilight hours. Being crepuscular, they are most active at dusk and dawn. They wake and nap frequently throughout the day.

Chinning: Rabbits have scent glands under their chins. Rabbits rub their chins on things (including other rabbits and their owners) to mark and claim things as their own or as part of their territory.

Do not allow your rabbits to share the same enclosure until you are certain they are compatible and will not fight.

Standing up: Rabbits stand up on their haunches when they are curious. They also stand up to scan the area for dangers or sometimes to beg for a treat from their owners.

Play behavior: Leaping and jumping in the air, kicking sideways, head shaking, and body twisting in the air while jumping are a combination of play motions referred to by scientists as *frisky hops*, and by rabbit lovers as *binkies*, or *dancing*. These movements are also a way young rabbits in the wild practice and perfect escape maneuvers they may have to use as adults. Other rabbit play behavior includes pushing or pawing at objects, carrying toys around in their mouths, and using their mouths to toss things into the air.

Affectionate behavior: Well-socialized and affectionate rabbits will seek out the compan-ionship of their owners. They enjoy being held, petted, or cuddled. They may lick their own-ers or nudge or even lightly nip to draw their owner's attention.

Aggressive behavior: Rabbits may lunge, snort, hiss, scratch, kick, and bite. They act this way if they are frightened, feel threatened, or are protecting their territory (territorial behavior). They may also be protecting their offspring (parental behavior, such as a doe protecting her kits) or protecting their posses-sions or resources (resource guarding).

Courtship behavior in bucks includes rapidly circling the doe, elevating his hind quarters, flagging his tail or laying his tail flat against his back, walking about stiff legged, and spray-ing urine on the doe.

Dominant behavior: Urine spraying, mount-ing, placing the head on top of the subordinate

Preventing or Managing Problem Behaviors

Problem Behavior	Ways to Prevent or Manage Problem
Urine spraying	Neuter or spay, reduce stress levels for frightened animals
Aggressive behavior	Neuter or spay
Territorial behavior	Neuter or spay
Hair pulling due to pregnancy or pseudopregnancy	Spay
Barbering	Correct the diet to provide sufficient fiber
Excessive digging and chewing	These behaviors are often caused by boredom. Excessive chewing may also be caused by a diet that does not contain adequate fiber. Visit and interact with your pet frequently every day. Provide play space, safe chew toys, and places to dig. Block off areas so that your rabbit cannot chew, dig, or destroy valuables, furniture, or carpets. If your rabbit is not receiving enough fiber in her diet, correct the diet accordingly. Make sure your pet always has plenty of fresh hay available at all times.
Aggressive behavior or fear behavior	Spend lots of time in kind, social interactions with your rabbit from the time she is a young bunny. Handle your rabbit carefully and correctly so you do not accidentally drop or injure your pet.
Failure to use the litter box	Urine spraying and fecal scattering are dominance and territorial behaviors that are often solved by neutering. In addition, you may add more litter boxes to your rabbit's environment. Be sure to place the litter boxes in areas where your pet has already chosen to eliminate.

animal's head, and barbering (pulling out hair) of subordinate animals are all forms of dominant behavior.

Foot thumping: Rabbits thump their feet in warning, fear, anger, or displeasure or as an alarm when they feel threatened or endangered.

Freezing in place: When rabbits "freeze" and remain motionless, they are afraid. They are trying to avoid detection by possible predators.

Hair pulling or self-barbering: Does that are pregnant or having a false pregnancy may pull their own hair from their dewlap, forelegs, and lower part of their chest and hips and use the hair to build nests. This behavior does not occur in does that have been spayed. Rabbits that do not receive enough fiber in their diets may also barber their own fur.

Lying down: A rabbit that lies on her side or abdomen with legs extended behind or out to the side of the body, or that lies upside down with her legs in the air is happy and feels relaxed, confident, and secure.

Squatting: A rabbit that is squatting with her hind limbs tucked underneath and ears laid back in repose is calm and comfortable.

Ear positioning can reveal whether a rabbit is relaxed, inquisitive and listening, or frightened.
- Ears laid back in repose: relaxed
- Ears forward: alert and listening
- Ears turned in different directions: alert and listening to sounds from more than one direction
- Ears laid back tight against the head: fear or submission, often noted together with the animal avoiding eye contact

Grooming and licking: When a rabbit grooms herself or another rabbit, she is relaxed and content. Grooming and licking are often signs of affection.

Tail flagging: Rabbits flag their tails as a form of communication and during breeding and courtship rituals.

Eating fecal pellets: Rabbits usually consume fecal pellets (cecotropes) in the evening when they feel safe and are not disturbed. (In the wild, cecotropes are consumed underground in the warren.)

Fecal scattering is territorial behavior. When a rabbit scatters her feces, rather than defecating in the usual location(s) or in the litter box, she is marking her territory. When a new rabbit is introduced into a home where a rabbit is already living, the established rabbit may claim the home as her territory by scattering her feces.

Urine spraying most commonly occurs in intact bucks toward subordinate males. Urine spraying can be a form of dominant aggression toward other bucks. Bucks may also spray does with urine during courtship (called enuration). When urine is sprayed, it is ejected backward. Some bucks may spray humans if they are attached or bonded to them. Neutering prevents or eliminates this natural behavior in males. Urine spraying, by both bucks and does,

Angora rabbits need more grooming than rabbits with short fur.

can occur when the animal is frightened or stressed.

Problem Behavior or Natural Behavior?

Rabbit "problem behaviors" are often simply natural rabbit behaviors that are problems for rabbit owners because they are undesirable behaviors (such as urine spraying) and owners do not know how to prevent or manage the situation. Problem behaviors are easier to prevent than correct. Not all problem behaviors can be anticipated, and every animal and situation is different. Fortunately, many problem behaviors can be prevented or managed successfully.

Always make sure that any unwanted behavior isn't caused by a medical condition. For example, a sick rabbit, or a rabbit in pain, may not behave naturally. She may be withdrawn, shy, or possibly act aggressively in self-defense. Like most prey species, rabbits try to hide their illness so they can hide their vulnerability. Check your rabbit daily to make sure she does not have any health problems!

Digging and chewing are normal rabbit behaviors. Rabbits should be given a secure play space and safe toys so they have opportunities to dig and chew. For example, to avoid the problem of having your rabbit dig in the carpet, give her something safe to dig, such as a hay mat. Additionally, do not allow her on your carpet. (Ingesting carpet fibers can cause

Remember

It is always best to do everything possible to prevent problem behavior, or a potential problem situation, rather than trying to correct it.

The rabbit's ears were tattered and torn when she was the victim of a dog attack. Always keep your rabbit away from other pets that can injure her.

problems such as choking and gastrointestinal obstruction.) To prevent your rabbit from chewing valuables (such as furniture, chair legs, and fabrics), give her safe chew toys. Block off areas of the home (with an exercise pen, barrier, or baby safety gate) where your bunny could do damage.

Socialization and handling: Many problem behaviors are due to lack of adequate socialization and handling when the animal was young or lack of attention and social interactions when the animal is mature. Some are caused by a bad experience the rabbit may have had. For example, if the rabbit was mishandled, dropped, or injured at some time, she could be fearful of being picked up or restrained. You must handle your pet

conditioning if these become necessary. Animal shelters and rabbit clubs often have counselors who know and understand rabbit behavior well and who may also be able to assist you with managing your bunny's behavior.

Discipline: Some authors have suggested managing behavior problems with disciplinary actions, such as pressing the animal's head downward to establish dominance, making screeching or other loud noises for distraction, or spraying the animal with water. These punitive measures are of questionable value and may actually frighten the animal or reinforce the unwanted behavior. A lot of rabbit behavior is instinctive. Much of her defensive behavior is for self-protection and self-preservation. Certainly, treating a rabbit unkindly or frightening her will only cause the animal to be more fearful and less trusting of humans. These actions risk breaking the bond of trust and affection that might have existed between the rabbit and her owner.

Every animal is different, and every situation must be carefully considered. Understanding a rabbit's behavior is the first step in having compassion for the animal. Rabbits do many of the things they do because they are a prey species that focus on survival. They frighten easily, panic quickly, and cannot tolerate prolonged stress. In fact, too much stress can cause shock and death in some rabbits. Discipline that might seem mild for one species can be very traumatic for a rabbit. For example, rabbits are not a predator species like dogs. The way rabbits think, their behaviors, and their instincts are very different. Discipline methods that might be successful for dogs are not necessarily appropriate or recommended for rabbits.

kindly and gently. Interact with her every day, starting from the time she is a young bunny. Often, hand feeding a small special treat, such as a dark leafy green, a sprig of parsley, or cilantro, will help reinforce bonding, promote confidence, and reward and encourage good behavior.

For complicated behavioral problems, consult a specialist. Veterinary behavioral specialists as well as veterinarians who specialize in exotic animal medicine can help you with advice regarding techniques in behavior modification, including desensitizing and counter-

Understanding rabbit behavior helps owners and rabbits live together happily. If you give your rabbit lots of love, attention, socialization, and environmental enrichment from the time she is very young, she will have a good chance of growing up to be a remarkable rabbit role model!

Vocalizations

Rabbits make different vocalizations, each with its own meaning. It is important to be able to recognize and understand the sounds your rabbit makes, so you will know if she is frightened, stressed, in pain, or simply content.

Rabbit Vocalizations

Sound	Meaning
Low, mild tooth grinding or light dental vibrations with whiskers quivering; purring; clicking; clucking	Contentment
Loud tooth grinding or crunching sounds	Pain or aggressive, threatening behavior
Tooth chattering	Pain
Sniff, wheeze, nasal sounds	Annoyance, protest, or friendly communication, depending on the circumstances
Grunting	Stressed, angry
Growling	Aggression, threatening
Snorting	Aggression, threatening
Honking	Sounds associated with breeding behavior of a buck, made when he is interested in mating with a doe in his presence. This sound can also be made by rabbits courting or by a rabbit asking for a treat.
Whimper	Usually made by pregnant or pseudopregnant does when they do not want to be disturbed, picked up, or removed from their nest box or cage
Scream	Extreme fear or pain
Squeal/scream	Natural vocalization made by buck immediately after breeding, usually accompanied by the buck falling over onto his side

Handling your rabbit safely is one of the most important things to learn so you can protect her from injury and also protect yourself from being scratched. Rabbits are afraid of falling or being lifted. If your pet feels insecure, she may panic or struggle to escape your hold. Most rabbit accidents occur during handling when a rabbit struggles, twists, is dropped, or falls. The most common injuries to rabbits resulting from these accidents are broken backs and limbs. Broken legs are difficult to treat in rabbits because of their delicate bones. Spine fractures result in permanent paralysis of the hindquarters.

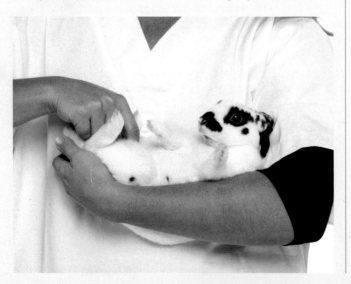

You must handle and restrain your rabbit very carefully to prevent injury!

Transport Long Distance

When you are transporting your pet a long distance, use a travel crate or a bunny stroller. These are the safest methods.

Transport Short Distance

When transporting your rabbit a short distance, you have 2 options.

1. Cradling (Bunny Bundling Method)

2. Hide-the-Head Method (Football-Carrying Method)

You can cradle your rabbit to carry her. Use one hand to grasp the loose skin at the back (scruff) of your pet's neck firmly but gently. At the same time, use your other hand to control back leg movement and to support your pet's feet and underside with your forearm.

Do not let your rabbit's rear legs dangle while you carry her! Cradle your rabbit's back against your side or abdomen.

You can instead use the hide-the-head method to carry your rabbit a short distance. Use one hand to grasp the loose skin at the back of your pet's neck firmly but gently. At the same time, use your other hand to control back leg movement and to support your pet's feet and underside with your forearm. Do not let your rabbit's rear legs dangle while you carry her! Next tuck your rabbit's head between your arm and the side of your body, as though you were carrying a footfall. Your pet will be facing the opposite direction you are facing. Your rabbit's head and eyes will be covered, and this will help keep her calm.

If you grasped the skin of the neck with your right hand, your rabbit's head will be tucked between your left arm and the left side of your body. If you grasped the skin

RABBIT

of the neck with your left hand, your rabbit's head will be tucked between your right arm and the right side of your body.)

Hypnotizing or Mesmerizing

To get a better look at your pet's underside, feet, genital area, cheeks, and teeth, you can put your bunny in a "hypnotic trance." To do this, grasp her firmly, but gently, by the skin over her withers with your left hand and support her hindquarters with your right hand. Hold her gently on her back in your lap. Gently tip her head backward, and speak to her calmly and soothingly. You can also gently pet her abdomen with the palm of your hand. Within a couple of minutes, your rabbit's breathing will slow and become deeper. Your pet's hind feet might start to tremble, but you can usually stop this by very lightly touching the feet. Your rabbit's eyelids will remain open during the time she is mesmerized.

"Rabbit hypnosis" lasts for only a short time period. Any sudden movements or loud noises will wake your pet suddenly out of her trance. So be prepared to support her body and handle her carefully so she does not become injured when she becomes alert again.

Syringe Feeding or Medicating

If you need to feed your rabbit liquid medication with a syringe, you can bundle her up in a towel, leaving only her head exposed, and place her onto a table on a nonslip mat. Gently but firmly place one arm around your pet, and hold her securely against your body while you feed her with the syringe. Be careful your rabbit doesn't try to struggle and escape. Rabbits do not like to have their mouths touched! Be sure to feed slowly and in small amounts from the syringe, giving your rabbit time to swallow so she does not aspirate fluid into her lungs.

Returning to Her Cage

When you place your pet back into her cage, always return her backward, with her hindquarters entering the cage first. Hold your rabbit so that she is facing you when you release her. This helps minimize the chances of her slipping, kicking, or being injured.

Important!

- Never lift a rabbit by her ears!
- Never let a rabbit's rear legs dangle while you carry her!
- Never lift a rabbit by her loin area or hind limbs, as this will cause violent thrashing and back injuries!
- Always maintain control of your rabbit. A frightened rabbit will instinctively kick out with her powerful hind legs and can seriously scratch her handler or twist, injure, and break her back! Rabbits will also try to jump off of tables.
- Always support your rabbit's hindquarters when you are carrying her.
- Always use a nonslip mat or heavy towel for your rabbit to sit on when you work with her on a tabletop. If the table surface is slippery, she may slip, struggle, or kick and break her back.
- Do not restrain your rabbit tightly around the neck for a long time. Prolonged restraint of this type occludes blood supply to the external jugular vein. This vein drains blood from the rabbit's head and eyes. If the external jugular vein is blocked for an extended period of time, the eyeballs will swell.

ACCOMMODATIONS FOR YOUR RABBIT

Understanding normal, natural rabbit behavior will give you insights into how to keep your rabbit content. You can do many things to make sure your rabbit has everything she needs to be healthy, happy, and safe in your home—and the best part is that all of these things are fun and easy to do!

Rabbit Essentials

There was a time, not that long ago, when most people kept their pet rabbits outside in a wire-bottom hutch or elevated cage. Many of these animals had little social interactions with their human caregivers. They were pulled out of their hutches when someone wanted to visit with them and then shelved away for long periods of time, with little human contact except the brief time it took to feed and water them. Rabbits housed under these conditions rarely had the chance to show anyone how smart and personable a rabbit can be! By comparison, if we treated our other family pets, such as dogs and cats, in the same manner—with little companionship or social enrichment—it would be considered cruelty. Before long, they would develop serious behavioral problems.

Fortunately, today more rabbits than ever live indoors as house pets. House rabbits are very entertaining, affectionate companions.

They have interesting lives, too. House rabbits spend more time interacting with the family and watching home activities. They are also much healthier than rabbits housed outdoors because they are not subjected to the stresses of outdoor living, such as predators, disease exposure, parasites (flies, mosquitoes, and ticks), and harsh weather (especially heat). If you want to give your rabbit the best home and care possible, seriously consider making her a house rabbit, rather than housing her permanently outside in a rabbit hutch. Indoor living is safer for your pet and makes it possible for you to spend more time with her and enjoy her more.

Your rabbit needs a cage large enough to allow her to be active, stretch out, lie down, sit up, hop about, and explore. The cage must also be large enough to accommodate all of your pet's accessories. As a general rule, the cage should be at least four times the size of your rabbit.

In addition to a sufficiently large cage habitat, your rabbit needs protected, bunny-proofed spaces where she can run, play, and investigate her surroundings. These areas may include a hallway in the house, an enclosed area in an extra bedroom, or space in the yard or patio sheltered from sun and predatory animals. When given access to long stretches of space, like a hallway, rabbits will run the length of the hallway in play. In a smaller, square-spaced area, they are more likely to dart and dash short distances when they play.

Rabbits are easy to please. Depending on your lifestyle and the amount of time and space you have available, you can create a housing setup for your bunny that is convenient, easy to clean, and as complex or simple as you want. Rabbits don't need much to turn their habitat into "home sweet home." They can adapt to a wide variety of housing, but they do have a few basic requirements. Fortunately, these things are easy and inexpensive to provide. As long as your rabbit has plenty of space to play safely, relax, explore, hide, sleep, and accommodate all the necessary essentials, your rabbit will be happy!

Rabbit Essentials

✔ Dry, clean, safe, comfortable housing
✔ Quiet, stress-free places to hide and sleep
✔ Space to run, play, and explore
✔ Hideaways
✔ Board and fake fleece to rest on and to protect the bottom of feet
✔ Litter boxes with clean litter
✔ Comfortable temperature and humidity, adequate ventilation
✔ Water bottles, crocks, feeders, hayracks
✔ Safe things to chew, a variety of toys, and interesting activities for social enrichment

Housing Considerations

There are some important things to keep in mind when deciding how to house your bunny.

1. Rabbits are very social animals. So you should house at least two rabbits together unless you have a lot of free time to spend and interact with your pet to keep her company and prevent loneliness and boredom.

2. Males and females should be neutered and spayed.

3. Animals should be compatible before they are housed together. Do not house males together.

4. Cages should be fabricated of smooth, corrosion-resistant, non-toxic material that is impervious to liquids and moisture and can be easily cleaned and sanitized.

5. Wire mesh cage floors can cause foot sores and foot ulcerations, especially in large or overweight rabbits. For comfort, use a solid floor cage or a cage with a floor pan for your rabbit. If you use wire for the cage flooring, the wire mesh should be 1 inch by 1 inch (2.54 cm by 2.54 cm). Rabbits housed on wire floors should always have a solid surface to sit on to rest their feet, such as a board covered by linoleum or fiberglass-reinforced plastic glued to wood with surface bumps for traction. You can also use a heavy plastic floor protector (smooth side up), such as those used under office chairs. A blanket made of false fleece or a comfortable chew-proof mat may also serve as a comfortable resting place. Avoid using crinkle wire mesh. This is even more damaging to rabbit feet than regular wire mesh.

6. Rabbit teeth grow throughout life, and chewing is an important, natural, necessary rabbit activity. Use only safe materials for caging, housing, bedding, and accessories. Your

Never allow your rabbit to run loose in the home or yard without supervision.

rabbit will chew on anything you put into the cage or play area! Do not use items made of hard plastic that can break into small pieces, materials made of fibers that can cause choking or obstruct the gastrointestinal tract, or woods that are chemically treated that may be toxic to rabbits.

7. Toys and activities are important to help prevent boredom. Boredom leads to behavioral problems, such as excessive and destructive chewing, or fur chewing and fur pulling.

8. Your rabbit needs a cage for confinement to use as a secure den.

9. Your rabbit also needs bunny proof, safe play areas in which to explore outside of her cage.

10. Rabbits are good escape artists. So the walls of your rabbit's play enclosures should fasten securely and be high enough to prevent escape.

Housing and Play Space Options

The cage, style, materials, and size you choose for your rabbit's housing will depend on the amount of space available in your home—and your imagination. Pet stores offer a wide variety of rabbit cages. You can also construct a custom cage of your own design. The most important things are for the cage to fit your pet's needs and to be convenient for you to reach your rabbit and reach inside the cage comfortably to feed, water, and clean.

When you select or build a cage, consider comfort as well as function. For example, do you prefer to stand up and reach inside of your pet's cage? If so, the cage will have to be on a support that is high enough to be the right height for you. The depth of the cage you select should be about arm's length, or 2½ feet deep (76 cm). This means that the cage will be longer than it is deep.

If you prefer to reach into the cage from the top, to prevent having to stoop or bend over the cage should be on a support to make it a convenient height for you. Think about what size your bunny will be when she is an adult. It's easy to lift a small rabbit through the top

Cage Options

Housing/ Cage Style	Advantage	Disadvantage	Make Sure
Wire cages	Easy to observe rabbit, well ventilated, easy to clean, door at top or side for convenience	Wire mesh floors can cause foot sores, so buy a cage with a solid bottom or provide your pet with a solid platform to rest her feet	If the floor is made of wire, the wire should be 1 inch × 1 inch (2.54 cm × 2.54 cm). Make sure wires are not made from or coated by toxic metals
Wooden Cages or hutches	Easy to build to any specifications, inexpensive	Porous and difficult to disinfect or sanitize, animal may chew the wood	Do not use cedar or chemically treated or toxic woods; do not coat with paints or varnishes

Play Space Options

Types of Play Space	Details
Exercise pens, X-pens (puppy pens)	Spacious, very versatile, easy to use, can be moved around and set up in various shapes, can be enlarged simply by clipping more panels together, panels fold together conveniently when not in use, come in various heights, some have doors that open on the side for convenience. Wire tops and shade covers may also be purchased that are custom made to fit X-pens. You can easily sit inside the pen to visit with your pet.
Children's hard plastic wading pools and hard plastic play yards for toddlers	Easy to clean and sanitize, easy to relocate, spacious enough to accommodate accessories and toys
Wire shelving	14 inch (35.5 cm) squares available from stores, clip together easily into any size or design, inexpensive
Baby gates	Safety gates that can be used to close off an area so that rabbit has full access to a room or hallway

of a cage. However, if your bunny is a large breed, she may be heavy and difficult to lift as an adult. In this case, a cage that opens from the front may be a better option.

In addition to single-level cages, you can purchase or design cages that have two or three levels. Rabbits enjoy using ramps and step-ups. This style of caging gives your pet more living space without taking up additional floor space.

Location and Environment

Where you place your pet's cage is an important decision. It depends on your home activity and lifestyle. Ideally, the cage should be placed where you can observe and enjoy your bunny and where she can watch family activities when she is awake and interested in her surroundings. Of course, she should always have hideaways in her cage where she can retreat to if she does not want to be disturbed! Rabbits like to be on the lookout, so don't obstruct your pet's view by blocking her cage with furniture and walls. She wants to see what's going on!

Temperature: Ideal housing temperature for rabbits is from 60 to 70°F (15.5 to 21.1°C). Rabbits are able to tolerate lower temperatures with gradual acclimation. However, they cannot tolerate warm temperatures and should not be housed in temperatures exceeding 80°F (26.6°C).

Do not place your rabbit's home enclosure near heaters, fireplaces, furnaces, fans, or in areas of direct sunlight.

Humidity should ideally be maintained between 45 and 55 percent. You can purchase an inexpensive hygrometer to measure the humidity in your home.

Do not place your rabbit's home in drafty areas where your pet could develop respiratory infections and pneumonia.

Ventilation: Adequate ventilation is important. At least three sides of your pet's cage should be wire to allow adequate ventilation. Do not use large aquaria for housing your pet, as these do not provide enough ventilation. Rabbits can also overheat in them.

Lighting: Place your rabbit's cage in an area of the house that is lighted during the day (ideally with some natural light) and dark at night.

Rabbits have excellent hearing and are stressed and startled by loud noises. Place your rabbit's home in a quiet place. Avoid areas of noisy activity or loud sounds such as doorbells, chiming clocks, barking dogs, televisions, sound systems, vacuum cleaners, and other appliances.

Rabbit hair, dander, and cage bedding can cause allergies in some people who have prolonged exposure to them, so physicians encourage not having pets and their cages in the bedroom. After all, if you are sleeping, you aren't visiting with your pet, so why be exposed to potential allergens during that time? The living room, den, or your office might be a more suitable place to put your rabbit's cage.

Accessories

In addition to safe, comfortable, escape-proof housing and play areas, your rabbit needs the following items.

1. A comfortable platform or washable rug to sit on to rest her feet. Baby blankets and false fleece work well. Avoid using terry cloth towels because they have loops than can unravel and your rabbit may eat the fibers.

2. A litter box with a natural-based, plant-based, or paper-based litter. Do not use clumping litter as it can get into nasal passages and

The litter box should be large enough to accommodate your rabbit and contain safe litter.

genital areas and can cause gastrointestinal obstruction if eaten.

3. Hanging water bottle (glass preferred, plastic acceptable if the bottle is hung outside the cage) with metal sipper tube

4. Heavy, nonspill ceramic crocks for food or feeder. If you use a J-shaped feeder, check that fine particles are not caked in the bend of the feeder, stopping the flow of pellets and preventing your rabbit access to the pellets.

5. Hanging hay rack

6. Houses and hideaways

7. Safe chew toys and chew sticks

8. A variety of safe, interesting toys for chewing, nudging, and tossing such as tunnel tubes, untreated wicker baskets, cardboard boxes, a pan of newspapers to dig up, hay stuffed in a cardboard or PVC tube, an empty paper bag, a paper bag stuffed with grass hay, a big tub of hay in which to dig and play. Often the simplest and cheapest things make the most interesting toys for rabbits. For example, a simple shower curtain ring attached to the wall of the cage will provide your rabbit with hours of entertainment. Your rabbit's toy box collection is limited only by your imagination!

9. Travel cage/travel kennel. Always keep your rabbit's travel cage prepared and ready in case an emergency trip to the veterinarian is necessary.

Optional Accessories

Portable play pens give your pet a safe place to play when you travel.

Remember

All enclosures should be in a safe location away from other animals and small children.

Important!

Rabbits must be caged when sick or injured, or when introducing new animals.

Harness and leash: Many rabbits enjoy going outside on a leash. Keep your rabbit in a safe area where you know there are no contaminants or toxic chemicals, such as pesticides or fertilizers, on the grounds. Using a portable playpen is safer when you take your bunny to the park to play.

Bunny stroller: Pet strollers are available from pet stores and rabbit specialty stores.

Pet strollers are a fun way to take your rabbit on an outing.

YOUR RABBIT COMES HOME

At last! You've found the perfect rabbit and it's time to bring her home! There are still some things left to do to make sure your pet's trip home is pleasant and that she will quickly adapt to her new family and home.

Get Ready!

Purchase housing, food, travel crate, supplies, accessories, and toys in advance. Have everything all ready and set up *before* you bring your bunny home. Take home some of the same food the breeder or pet store has been feeding your bunny to prevent stress and gastrointestinal upset due to a sudden change in diet.

Set up housing, enclosures, and accommodations in advance so that when you arrive home, you can transfer your pet directly into her new environment. If you do so, she won't have to wait, confused and uneasy, in the travel crate while you prepare everything.

Bunny Proofing Your Home

Before you bring your pet home, check for possible hazards a busy bunny could encounter if she were to escape accidentally. Your home can be a dangerous place for a runaway rabbit.

Lower yourself to your pet's eye level to take a good look. Many accidents are waiting to happen in your home. If you can find them, you can prevent them!

Electrical cords: Your rabbit will be tempted to chew on anything she finds. If she chews on an electrical cord, she could suffer electrical shock and possibly start a fire in your home. If your rabbit escapes, immediately unplug all electrical cords until you find her.

For full-time prevention in your home, you can use vinyl tubing or small-diameter PVC tubing to cover the electrical cords permanently. Simply slice the vinyl or PVC tubing lengthwise, and insert the electrical cords inside of it.

Use outlet covers, such as those sold for toddler safety, to cover the electrical outlets.

Cords for curtains and blinds: Make sure your bunny does not have access to curtain and blind cords. She could become entangled or strangled in them.

Traps and bait: Remove all rodent traps, poisonous rodent and insect baits, and poisons from your home. They are as deadly for your rabbit as they are for vermin!

Household chemicals: Rabbits can nudge, paw, and open and enter cabinets. Do not keep household products such as cleaning agents, pesticides, paints, fertilizers, and other poisonous chemicals in low cabinets where your rabbit can get to them. Either install child-proof locks on low cabinets or move your household products to your wall cabinets.

Other animals: Keep your rabbit separated and safe from other pets that can harm her. When you are not home, keep her safe in her cage in the house. Never leave your rabbit unsupervised outside or on a patio where she can fall victim to birds of prey, neighborhood dogs, or wild animals.

Outside doors: Make sure all doors to the outside or the garage are closed. If your rabbit escapes to the garage, she will be exposed to additional hazards and poisons such as anti-freeze (ethylene glycol), which is a deadly, sweet tasting poison that causes rapid kidney failure.

If your rabbit escapes outside, it will be difficult, if not impossible, to find her. She will certainly not survive the dangers of traffic, neighborhood and wild animals, and harsh weather conditions (especially heat).

Poisonous plants: While your rabbit is on the loose, she will forage for food. Unfortunately, many house and garden plants are poisonous, as are fertilizers and cocoa mulch. Remove all poisonous items from the area, or block off the area, until you retrieve your rabbit.

The Trip Home

Prepare the travel crate and give your rabbit time to get used to it. Take your rabbit straight home from the breeder's or the pet store. Turn down the sound on the radio so you don't disturb your pet. You can cover the travel crate with a thin towel or blanket to help reduce frightening car sounds. Do not stop and leave your car with your rabbit in it, especially on a hot day. On a warm day, the temperature inside a car can quickly soar above 120°F (49°C) within a few minutes, even with the windows cracked

Common Poisonous Plants

Aconite (monkshood, wolfsbane)	Birdseye primrose	Daily	Oleander
	Blue cardinal flower (*Lobelia*)	Foxglove (*Digitalis*)	Onion
Amaryllis		Hydrangea	Philodendron
American holly	Buttercup (*Ranunculus*)	Iris	Poinsettia
American nightshade		Lily (several species of lily)	Rhododendron
Angel's trumpet	Crocus		Tulip
Azalea	Chrysanthemum	Lupine	Yew
Bird of paradise	Daffodil	Mistletoe	

Note: This is a list of more common poisonous plants. However, this list is not all-inclusive. Many other plant species may be harmful or toxic to rabbits.

open and the car parked in the shade. You rabbit would quickly overheat and die.

Quiet, Please!

When you bring your rabbit home, place her into her enclosure in a quiet area where she can comfortably hide, sleep, and recover from the stresses of being transported and changing environments. When she is ready to visit and explore, talk to her softly, gently caress her, and offer her a healthy treat, such as a sprig of parsley. She will need time to adapt to her new home and to get to know you.

If Your Rabbit Escapes

Rabbits are escape artists. They can dig out from under enclosures, clamber over them, and squeeze through the tiniest of spaces. If they manage to get their head through an opening, they can wriggle their bodies through, too. Rabbits are also very fast! If your rabbit escapes and is panicked and flighty, it's unlikely that you can catch her. In fact, chasing her will add to her stress. She could injure herself running into and bouncing off of walls and obstacles. If you can close off the area surrounding your pet, do so quickly. Try to reassure your pet to calm her. Put her favorite tasty treats into her cage and hideaways. Leave the door open for her to return. You can also set up areas with hideaways and treats and then surround them with an X-pen. Leave an opening between the panels for your pet to enter. Be on guard to close the panels as soon as your pet returns and enters your trap.

If your rabbit has escaped outside, don't expect her to come home on her own. You will have to search for her actively. Be prepared to catch her when you find her. A tightly woven

If your rabbit escapes, she can find many common chemicals and poisons in your home, garage, and garden.

fishing net on a long handle can be very helpful in case your rabbit decides to bolt and flee. If you do not have a net, you can use a small sheet or large towel to throw over your rabbit and bundle her up before you transport her to her cage.

If you can't find your rabbit, don't give up. You can purchase one or more small humane traps at the local pet store or feed store (Havahart live trap). Bait the traps with your rabbit's favorite treats, and put them into areas that are shaded all day. Check the traps several times a day.

You are most likely to catch your rabbit in the evening or early morning hours when she is most active. You rabbit will surely be hungry, thirsty, and very frightened when you find her. Check your pet for signs of injury. Give her food, water, and time to recover from her adventures.

Rabbits are meticulously clean animals. In fact, if your rabbit stops grooming herself, it is a sign that she is not feeling well and that something is wrong.

Grooming helps keep your pet's coat beautiful, clean, and free of mats. Grooming spreads natural oils in the coat, keeps the skin healthy and free of parasites and debris, and removes dander and loose hair. This reduces the amount of hair your rabbit will swallow during self-grooming. Ingested hair forms into hairballs in the digestive tract and can cause illness.

Grooming sessions are a wonderful way to strengthen your bond of friendship! The more you handle and interact with your rabbit, the easier she will be to groom. Start getting your pet used to being handled and groomed from the time she is a bunny. Even if there isn't a lot to groom when your pet is a youngster, your bunny will enjoy the attention and will learn to adapt to being touched, cared for, and groomed.

Rabbits do not need baths. In fact, rabbits do not like baths and find them to be very stressful. Rabbits can panic, struggle, and be injured if they are submerged in water. In addition, bathing removes the beneficial natural oils in a rabbit's coat. Rabbit coats can retain water and are difficult to dry, making the animal prone to becoming chilled and developing respiratory problems.

Short Hair

If your rabbit has short hair, dampen a soft cloth to wipe the surface of the coat gently to remove flyaway hairs, excess dander and remove static electricity before you start. Use a soft bristle brush to brush out the coat gently. Then wipe the coat again with a damp cloth to pick up the remaining dander and hair.

Long Hair or Wool

Depending on the breed, hair type, hair length, and amount of shedding, long hair may need to be groomed often to prevent mats from forming, especially on the underside of the body. Flea combs, pin brushes, and soft bristle brushes are all useful tools in maintaining the coat. (Slicker brushes are not recommended as they can injure a rabbit's sensitive skin).

Start with the ends of the hair, and separate them carefully. Then gradually advance to the base of the hair, at the skin. Comb the hair carefully and gently. Do not pull!

Ears

Rabbits with short hair do not need to have the hair on their ears groomed. It can be lightly wiped with a dampened cloth. For rabbits with lots of hair on their ears, such as Angora rabbits, handle the ears gently. Comb or brush the hairs very gently. The skin on the ears is delicate and very sensitive, so be careful!

Check the inside of the ears for wax buildup. You can gently clean any wax or dirt away using a soft, slightly moistened cotton swab. If the ear is sore, dry, or crusty, add mineral oil to the cotton swab. Do not allow water or oil to drip down the ear canals. Do not push the cotton swab, wax, or debris down into the ear canal. If you see signs of parasites or infection, such as sores, crusting, or redness (see "Health") contact your veterinarian right away.

Toenails

To trim nails, grasp the skin at the back of the neck

RABBIT

(nape, scruff) with one hand. Support the hindquarters securely with the other hand. Rest the rabbit's back firmly against your abdomen (see "How-To: Handling"). Trim only the tips of the nails where there is no blood supply.

To protect your rabbit from injury during restraint and to make sure you learn how to trim her toenails safely, ask your veterinarian or groomer to demonstrate nail trimming before you try to do it yourself.

Grooming Tips!

1. Groom your rabbit once a week or more often if necessary.

2. Keep grooming sessions short and enjoyable. Stop grooming before your rabbit becomes bored or agitated! If your pet needs extensive grooming, break it up into several short sessions over several days.

3. Make it fun! Reward your pet for good behavior with small bits of healthy treats, such as a sprig of parsley, throughout the grooming session.

4. Choose the right time! Groom your rabbit when you are relaxed and not in a hurry and when your pet is in a sociable mood. Don't bother her when she is trying to rest.

5. Make sure your rabbit feels secure, so she doesn't panic and try to escape. Make sure your rabbit cannot jump or fall from the table. If frightened, she may struggle or try to jump. She could injure or break her back or limbs.

6. Consider your comfort level. Place your rabbit onto a table at a comfortable level for you to work sitting or standing (whichever you prefer). Work in an area that is well lit and quiet, and where there are no distractions or things that may frighten your rabbit, such as other family pets.

7. To help your rabbit feel secure and to give you better control over her on the table, place a nonslip mat onto the grooming table. Keep your rabbit close to your body while you groom her.

8. Rabbit skin is very sensitive and thin. It is easily damaged. Be sure to use only soft grooming tools. Groom very gently to avoid skin injury such as tears and punctures.

9. Brush the hair before you comb it! Don't pull on the hair!

10. If your rabbit has a hair mat, tease it apart gently with a comb. It you cannot remove the mat, contact your veterinarian or groomer for help. The mat will have to be carefully teased out to prevent tearing the skin. Do not cut out the hair mat or shave the skin, as you could easily cut or burn your pet's skin!

11. Do not use shampoos or fragrances designed for humans on your rabbit.

12. Do not use flea shampoos or pesticide products on your rabbit that were developed for use in dogs. Consult with your veterinarian before using any kind of parasite control product on your rabbit.

Take advantage of the grooming session to perform a complete health check on your pet (see "Health"). Check her skin for lumps, bumps, sores, scabs, and parasites. Check her teeth, eyes, and ears, and also under the tail. Trim the toenails as needed. When you groom your rabbit, check her thoroughly from the nose to the toes!

Note that hair dryers are not recommended for rabbits. The noise can frighten them. Some hair dryers may make noise at a frequency that is stressful for rabbit ears and hearing range. Hair dryers may also burn a rabbit's delicate skin.

FEEDING YOUR RABBIT

A nutritionally balanced diet is absolutely essential to your rabbit's health. The most common health problems involve the gastrointestinal tract, and many of these can be fatal. Since you have full control over your pet's diet, you can easily prevent the majority of rabbit health problems simply by feeding your pet a wholesome diet.

Rabbits love to eat! Some rabbits are such eager eaters that they can become overweight if the diet is not balanced. Other rabbits can be finicky eaters and be very particular about their food preferences. These are often rabbits that have been spoiled with so many sweet treats that they turn their twitching noses up at good wholesome nutrition! These animals can sometimes be a challenge to get back on track. To keep your pet healthy, it's best to start out feeding your bunny the right foods, in the right amount—right from the very start!

Rabbit Digestive System

Rabbits are strict herbivores. This means they are vegetarians (they eat only plant materials). Rabbits have special behavioral, anatomical, and biological adaptations that influence their dietary needs. So their nutritional requirements differ from other herbivores.

Rabbits have an elaborate and remarkable digestive system that requires a coarse, high-fiber diet to function properly. High-fiber, nondigestible particles stimulate a rabbit's gastrointestinal motility, digestion, secretions, absorption, and excretion. This is why it is essential for rabbits to have fresh grass hay available at all times. Rabbits do not adapt well to limited feeding times. They have a very long, sensitive digestive tract that can be easily upset by a sudden change in diet or the wrong kinds of foods. Bacteria in the gut play an important role in how rabbits absorb nutrients. Rabbits consume and recycle some of their feces (cecotrophy). Rabbits are unable to vomit. Clearly, the rabbit's digestive system is quite different from that of other species, so let's take a look!

Mouth: The rabbit's teeth are designed for a high-fiber, herbivorous diet. Rabbits chew in a lateral (side to side) motion. Providing your pet with high-fiber hay to eat stimulates digestion and helps keeps the teeth worn correctly.

Stomach: The rabbit's stomach is simple, very large, and usually full of food at all times. The pyloric sphincter is muscular.

The intestines are very long—approximately 8 feet (2.4 m) of small intestines and 4 feet (6.2 m) of large intestines—more than 10 times longer than the animal's body!

The cecum is the largest part of the intestinal tract. It is 10 times the size of the stomach! The cecum separates and eliminates fiber. With the help of specific beneficial bacteria, the cecum ferments and concentrates ingested food (proteins, amino acids, and volatile fatty acids) so that these necessary energy substances can be absorbed by the animal. This hindgut fermentation also produces cecotropes (night feces). Cecotropes differ from the dry, hard fecal pellets passed during the day. They are soft pellets with a light green sheen, encased in mucus. They occur in small bunches and contain protein, B complex vitamins, vitamin K, dietary minerals, and crude fiber. Rabbits eat cecotropes directly from the anus in the early-morning hours. This normal, necessary behavior allows the animal to extract additional valuable nutrients. (Bunnies begin eating their mother's cecotropes at two weeks of age and their own cecotropes at about three weeks of age.) After cecotropes are ingested, they ferment in the stomach. Their recycled nutrients are absorbed from the small intestine. (By comparison, the cecum in humans is called the appendix. It is small and serves no essential purpose.)

Gastrointestinal transit time is relatively rapid in the rabbit and takes four to five hours.

Because rabbits cannot vomit, blockage of the stomach is often caused by improper diet and foreign body obstruction. Blockage can lead to a painful death caused by the accumulation of gas and liquids distending the stomach and compressing other body organs.

Feeding Habits

During their waking hours, rabbits love to forage for food. They find their food primarily through their keen senses of smell and touch to identify and discriminate their food. In the wild, rabbits consume large quantities of vegetation, grasses, hay, leaves, and roots. They will also eat coarse, nondigestible fiber such as dried bark and dried twigs.

You can take advantage of your rabbit's natural desire to forage by hiding special high-fiber, low-calorie treats in your pet's play area for her to find. Make it a game. Your pet will be sure to receive the extra fiber she needs, and she will have fun foraging for it. Providing your pet with high-fiber food, such as grass hay, gives her something enjoyable to do and helps prevent boredom.

Water

Because much of their diet consists of dry matter (hay and pellets), water is a critical component of your bunny's diet. Some rabbits prefer to drink from water bottles; others prefer to drink from heavy ceramic crocks or weighted stainless steel bowls.

Rabbits must drink a lot of water to remain well hydrated and to prevent gastrointestinal problems such as gut stasis. Under normal conditions, a rabbit will drink as much as a dog that weighs ten times the rabbit's body weight! Water intake varies according to the rabbit's diet, activity level, health, and environmental conditions. Measure your rabbit's water intake to be sure she is drinking enough.

On average, rabbits drink 1 to 2 teaspoons per 3.5 ounces (5 to 10 mL per 100 g) body weight. This is 2 to 5 ounces (50 to 150 mL), or more, of water daily. In other words, a rabbit drinks approximately 10 percent of her body weight daily. Rabbits can drink much more if the weather is warm or if they are very active, pregnant, or lactating.

If deprived of water, a rabbit will stop eating and can quickly develop hepatic lipidosis and die. Always have plenty of fresh, clean water available at all times. If your pet drinks

from a bottle, check daily to make sure that the sipper tube works and is not plugged.

What to Feed

Food is a powerful tool. By feeding your rabbit the right kinds of food in the right amounts, you can keep her healthy and prolong her life. You can also win her heart at the same time! When you offer food to your pet, you strengthen the friendship bond between you. Food can also be used as a training reward when you teach your bunny a trick, praise her

Remember

Always give your rabbit more water than you think she would normally drink in a day.

Your rabbit should have access to fresh grass hay at all times.

for good behavior, or try to bribe her to do the things you want her to do.

Feeding your rabbit a nutritious, well-balanced diet is easy. Just like people, every rabbit is a unique individual, so consider dietary needs on an individual basis. Feed your rabbit according to her nutritional requirements, age and stage of development, health, and activity level. In general, small breeds have faster metabolisms and higher caloric requirements per pound of body weight than large breeds. A nonbreeding adult rabbit eats approximately 5 percent of her body weight in completely dry diet. Sick or debilitated rabbits have greater nutritional needs. Very young bunnies and rabbits that are breeding, pregnant, or lactating also have increased dietary and caloric requirements. For example, a lactating doe needs two to three times the nutrition she needed before she was pregnant.

Rabbits need a high-fiber diet with at least 18 percent fiber (18 to 22 percent fiber is preferred). Low-fiber diets can cause gastrointestinal stasis and hepatic lipidosis. They can rapidly result in death.

Feed Only Fresh Food!

Be sure the food you feed your rabbit is fresh.

✔ Do not buy food that has been displayed in store windows. It can get hot and lose its nutritional value.

✔ Check the milling date on the package to verify the shelf life of the product. If there is no milling date, check for a statement that says "use before." Do not buy food within six weeks of its expiration date.

✔ Buy only as much food as your rabbit will eat in one month.

✔ Do not mix new food with old food.

✔ Throw away old pellets and hay that have become finely ground or have turned to dusty powder. This food has no nutritional value and may grow fungi and mold that are toxic to rabbits.

✔ Purchase hay that is specially packaged for feeding rabbits. Oxbow timothy hay or Oxbow orchard grass are good choices. Other types of grass hay include Bermuda, fescue, Sudan, brome, meadow, and buffalo. Legume hays are, for the most part, too rich in protein and should be avoided. (Alfalfa is a legume hay that may be fed to growing bunnies or debilitated animals.)

Be Aware

Bark and twigs that are not completely dry can contain substances toxic to rabbits.

Caution!

Make sure your rabbit eats only the right kinds of food and doesn't have access to the wrong things to nibble or chew!

✔ Do not buy hay designated for horse stalls or that has been stored in open, outdoor bins. These hays may be contaminated with mold, mildew, bird droppings, or urine, feces and germs from wild rodents.

What to Feed, How Much, and How Often

Grass hays: Fresh Timothy hay (or other local mixed grass hays, such as orchard hay and meadow hay) contain 18 to 22 percent fiber and are an excellent choice for hay. Choose long-strand hays for maximum fiber. Fresh grass hay is very important for digestion and should be available to all rabbits at all times. Rabbits should be allowed to eat as much grass hay as they want.

Alfalfa hay is suitable for younger, growing, active rabbits or for sick rabbits that have increased protein requirements. Alfalfa hay is not recommended for nonbreeding adult rabbits because it is high in calories and calcium and can lead to obesity and hypercalcemia, especially in sedentary animals. Consult with your veterinarian to determine how much your rabbit should receive and for how long, based on her health. Always have fresh grass hay available for your rabbit, even when you are feeding her alfalfa hay at the same time.

Commercial rabbit pellets: Pellets manufactured specifically for rabbits cover the animal's nutritional needs. Feed high-fiber pellets (18 percent fiber or higher). Generally, Timothy hay–based pellets are recommended for most healthy adult rabbits rather than alfalfa-based pellets. For adult, nonbreeding rabbits, the pellet protein content should not exceed 14 percent.

Buy pellets for your rabbit in small quantities (not more than your rabbit will eat in one month) so that the food you feed your rabbit is always fresh and doesn't spoil. Check the milling date on the bag to ensure that the product is fresh. Store the pellets in a clean, closed container in a cool, dry place.

Feeding Guidelines

For an adult nonbreeding rabbit, feed no more than 1/8 cup (30 g) of high-fiber maintenance Timothy hay–based pellet food per 5 pounds (2.27 kg) of the animal's body weight.

Commercial rabbit pellets meet your rabbit's nutritional needs and help cover all the nutritional bases. However, if you feed too many pellets, your rabbit can become obese.

Avoid pellets that contain whole seeds, nuts, grains, corn, and dried vegetables. They are fattening. They contain large amounts of starch and sugar that can cause serious digestive problems and even result in death.

Do not feed pellets free choice. Your rabbit could overeat and become overweight.

Do not feed pellets manufactured for other species.

Many rabbit owners contend that their rabbits do not need to be fed rabbit pellets as long as they have high-quality, high-fiber grass hay available at all times and a wholesome selection of fresh vegetables daily. Every animal's case is different. Be sure to discuss your rabbit's diet with your veterinarian to develop

the best menu for your rabbit based on her
age, health, and activity level.

Vegetables: Offer your rabbit at least three
kinds of fresh dark-green or dark-yellow vegetables daily, such as arugula, parsley, cilantro, basil, beet greens, broccoli leaves, collard
greens, radichio, dandelion leaves, kale, carrot
tops, and dark-green leafy lettuces, such as
romaine lettuce. Feed at least 1 cup (240 g) of
leafy vegetables for every 4 pounds (1.8 kg)
of your pet's body weight.

Rinse vegetables well before feeding them
to your rabbit. Remove all old vegetables from
the cage daily so they do not spoil.

If you wish to add carrots to your bunny's
diet, feed them sparingly. Carrots are high in
sugar and carbohydrates. If your rabbit eats
too many, carrots can cause serious gastrointestinal problems, including stasis.

Fruits: Offer your rabbit a small amount
of high fiber, fresh fruit daily. Limit fruit to
1 to 2 tablespoons/15 to 30 mL (not to exceed
1/2 ounce/14 g) per 5 pounds (2.27 kg) of
body weight. Remove all seeds and pits before
feeding fruits. Limit fruits to those containing
lower amounts of sugar, such as apple, peach,
plum, pear, pineapple, papaya, and melon.
You can also feed your rabbit very small
amounts of strawberry, blackberry, raspberry,
and blueberry.

If your rabbit is overweight, limit or elimi-
nate fruits from her diet until she has returned
to her ideal weight.

Harmful Foods to Avoid

Avoid feeding certain foods to your rabbit.

1. Starchy or toxic foods: beans, corn, peas,
potatoes, potato peelings (potato eyes contain
the toxin solanine), and rhubarb

2. Cooked, canned, preserved, or frozen
vegetables

3. Fruits with high sugar or starch content

4. Canned and dried fruits

5. Seeds, pits, nuts, whole grains

6. Candy, cookies, or other foods that are
sharp, sticky, and/or contain refined sugar

Grapes are poisonous to some animals.
Although grape and raisin toxicity hasn't been
documented to date in rabbits, it is safest to
avoid them. Some kinds of avocado hybrids are
toxic to animals, and because it is difficult to
know which kind you buy, it is safest not to
feed avocados to your pet.

Supplements

If you feed your rabbit a balanced,
nutritious diet, supplements and salt blocks
are not necessary. The fresh food you feed,
together with fresh grass hay and the commercial rabbit pellets, contain all the necessary ingredients for your pet's health. In fact,
unless your veterinarian prescribes a specific
supplement for your rabbit's diet, feeding
supplements could upset your rabbit's dietary
balance. Indiscriminate supplementation can
be harmful.

Feeding Tips

1. When in doubt, always ask your veterinarian to help you formulate a balanced diet
for your rabbit.

2. Examine your rabbit daily to make sure she is healthy, eating, drinking, urinating, defecating, and behaving normally.

3. Measure your rabbit's food and water. Keep track of how much she eats and drinks.

4. Weigh your rabbit every week. Keep a record book of her weight to make sure she is not gaining or losing too much weight.

5. Do not feed pellets free choice.

6. Feed only high-fiber, healthy foods and treats.

7. Never change your rabbit's diet suddenly. If a change is needed, make the change gradually to prevent gastrointestinal upset and illness.

Weighing In

Obesity is a serious health problem that can threaten your pet's life. If your rabbit has become overweight, take action right away to help your pet return to a normal weight and keep her healthy.

1. Weigh your rabbit weekly. Keep a record of her weight loss over time.

2. Do not put your rabbit on a crash diet. Weight loss must be very gradual. Your rabbit should lose about 1 percent of her body weight per week until she has returned to her ideal weight. This may take five to six months or more to accomplish, depending on how overweight your pet is.

Remember
Your bunny's dietary needs will change with her growth, weight, health, and activity level. Make dietary adjustments gradually!

If your rabbit refuses to eat, you may have to feed her with a syringe or eyedropper. Contact your veterinarian right away for guidance.

3. Do not feed sweet treats or high-calorie foods.

4. Do not feed pellets free choice.

5. Make sure fresh grass hay is available at all times.

6. Increase the amount of fiber in your rabbit's diet.

7. Give your pet lots of chew toys to prevent boredom and destructive chewing.

If your rabbit refuses to eat, it is likely that she has an underlying health problem that is suppressing her appetite. For example, she may have dental problems or sores in the mouth that make it difficult or painful to eat. Rabbits cannot go long without eating before they develop hepatic lipidosis, gastric stasis, and die. Contact your veterinarian immediately for help. Your veterinarian may recommend syringe feeding your rabbit Oxbow Critical Care for Herbivores. This special diet contains the correct amount of fiber and nutrition for sick or debilitated rabbits.

HEALTH

The most important health care you can give your rabbit is preventive health care. Preventing health problems is much easier than treating them!

Keeping Your Rabbit Healthy

The majority of common rabbit health problems can be easily prevented by feeding your pet the right diet; keeping her environment clean, comfortable, safe, and stress free; and careful handling. Check your rabbit every day for signs of illness. The sooner you detect and treat the problem, the better your bunny's chances are for recovery and a longer life.

Your rabbit may live up to eight years or more if you give her excellent care and a nutritious, balanced diet. However, if your rabbit becomes ill, she will need immediate help to make sure her condition does not worsen or become life threatening. This chapter gives you the information you need to prevent, recognize, and manage health problems so you can do your best to keep your rabbit healthy.

Rabbits are prey animals. Throughout their evolution, they have been hunted and eaten by carnivorous predator species. As a result, rabbits have developed instinctive behaviors and special anatomical and biological features

to help them survive (see "Introduction to the Rabbit" and "Understanding Your Rabbit"). When a rabbit senses the presence of a predator, her instinct is to sit still, camouflaged in her surroundings, to avoid detection. If this method of self-preservation fails, the rabbit will flee. A frightened rabbit on the run is capable of quick bursts of speed and has the ability to leap, turn, and change directions several times in an effort to escape. When a rabbit is sick or injured, she instinctively tries to conceal signs of pain or weakness so she does not appear vulnerable to predators. This stoic behavior increases a rabbit's chances of survival in the wild. Unfortunately, this same behavior makes it more difficult for us to tell when our domestic pet rabbits are sick. Sometimes a rabbit can hide her injury or illness so well that the problem is not noticed until it has become very serious. By then, treatment may be difficult and less likely to succeed.

If you think your rabbit is sick, contact your veterinarian right away for advice. Early diagnosis and treatment can make the difference between prolonged illness and good health. The sooner your pet's problem is detected, diagnosed, and treated, the better her chances are for recovery and the less she will suffer.

Signs of a Sick Rabbit

Some rabbits can hide signs of illness for a long time. However, many health problems are obvious, such as refusal to eat or drink, no longer self-grooming, difficulty breathing, diarrhea, constipation, lethargy, discharge from the eyes or nose, skin and ear sores, and weight loss.

Important Note About Rabbit Urine

Rabbit urine can be thick and appear creamy. The consistency and appearance varies according to the amount of calcium in a rabbit's diet and relates to the amount of calcium carbonate in the urine. Normal rabbit urine ranges in color from yellow to orange to rust

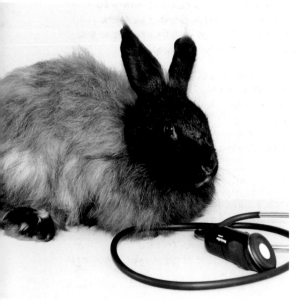

Important

Check your rabbit daily to make sure she is healthy and eating, drinking, urinating, defecating, and behaving normally.

due to various pigments. Reddish-colored urine does not necessarily indicate that blood is in the urine. Your veterinarian can test for blood in your rabbit's urine.

Signs of Pain

1. Tooth grinding, may scream if pain is severe

2. Refusal or inability to eat or drink, may drop food from mouth or drool

3. Reluctance to move

4. Abnormal body position, hunched position, head lowered

5. Unusually sensitive to touch

6. Rapid breathing, increased heart rate

Signs of Fear

1. Foot thumping, may growl

2. Rapid breathing, increased heart rate

3. Struggles to break loose from handler

4. Tries to escape

If Your Rabbit Is Sick

1. Rabbits are easily stressed. Isolate your sick rabbit in a comfortable, quiet area with subdued lighting away from other pets.

2. Contact your veterinarian immediately for advice.

3. To prevent the possible spread of infection, wash your hands thoroughly after handling your sick rabbit and before handing other pets or food.

Is Your Rabbit Healthy?

	Healthy Rabbit	Sick Rabbit
Appearance and attitude	Bright, alert, interested in surroundings, curious about new objects, playful	Dull expression, lethargic, depressed, abnormal body position or stance
Eyes	Bright, clear eyes with clean eyelids and lid margins	Discharge from eyes, cloudy eyes, eyes partially or completely closed, eyelids and lid margins red, swollen
Ears	Clean ears	Discharge from ears, crusty sores, redness, scratching at ears, head shaking, head tilt, parasites
Nose	Clean nose and nostrils	Discharge from nose, difficulty breathing
Mouth	Normal teeth and gums	Dental malocclusion, broken teeth, dental abscesses, mouth sores, drooling "slobbers," inability to eat, dropping food from mouth
Skin and coat	Healthy skin and coat	Areas of patchy hair loss, scabs, sores, lumps, masses, warts, abscesses, moist dermatitis (especially in dewlap), external parasites, pododermatitis (foot sores), barbering or hair pulling, or no longer self-grooming
Digestive system	Eating, drinking, digesting, and defecating normally	Lack of appetite, not drinking enough, diarrhea, constipation, unusually small fecal pellets, or abnormally large, doughy, or distended abdomen
Weight	Normal weight for breed and age	Too thin, overweight, or obese
Body stance	Normal body position, stance, movement, and coordination	Inability to sit, stand, or move normally; hunched body; head tilt; circling; uncoordinated; paresis; paralysis
Urogenital	Normal genitalia, normal urination	Blood in urine from bladder infection or calculi (stones), abnormal or bloody vaginal discharge, swollen testicles

4. Wash all housing, accessories, feeders, dishes, ceramic crocks, bottles, sipper tubes, and toys that were in contact with your sick rabbit.

5. When transporting your rabbit to the veterinary clinic, place a soft blanket onto the bottom of the travel carrier to keep her comfortable and prevent her from slipping or sliding. Cover the carrier with a light towel to reduce noise and bright light during the trip.

Helping Your Veterinarian Help Your Rabbit

Veterinary surveys report that rabbits are "the most popular exotic pet patient" seen in veterinary practices. You might not think your bunny is exotic, but rabbits differ in many ways from common domestic pet species, such as dogs and cats. Rabbits are popular pets, but they can be challenging patients. Not all veterinarians have extensive experience in rabbit medicine and surgery. Your local veterinary association or the Association of Exotic Mammal Veterinarians (see "Information") can help you find a veterinarian who has expertise treating rabbits. Select a veterinarian before you need one so you will not lose valuable time finding help in an emergency situation.

To make the most of the veterinary visit, prepare a list of concerns in advance that you want to discuss with the doctor. Your veterinarian will also ask you questions about your rabbit to understand and treat her better. The veterinarian may ask:
- When did you first notice the problem?
- Does your rabbit appear to be in any discomfort or pain?
- How old is your rabbit?

Be Careful!
Handle your rabbit very carefully when you examine her. Rabbits have very sharp nails and powerful hind limbs. They can inflict deep scratch wounds. If not restrained properly, you can be scratched and your rabbit can break her back or legs if she struggles and twists (see "How-To: Handling Your Rabbit").

- When did your rabbit last eat and drink?
- When did your rabbit last urinate and defecate, and what did it look like?
- What do you feed your pet and how much, including treats and supplements?
- Are there other animals at home? What species? If you have other rabbits, do any of them have similar problems?
- Does your rabbit have normal stools, diarrhea, or constipation?
- Has your rabbit gained or lost weight?
- Describe your pet's housing, handling, exercise, and play activities
- Has there been a recent change in your rabbit's diet or living environment?
- How long have you owned your pet?
- Where did you obtain your rabbit?
- Is your rabbit spayed or neutered, or has she had any surgeries in the past?
- If your rabbit is an intact female, is she pregnant? Has she ever produced a litter?
- Has your rabbit been exposed to any sick animals or harmful plants or chemicals?
- Has your rabbit had any previous health problems?

Don't worry if you don't have all the answers. Any information you can give your veterinarian will be very helpful.

Should Your Rabbit Be Neutered?

Unless you are planning on breeding your rabbit and are able to find loving homes for lots of bunnies, it is wise to neuter your pet. A neutered rabbit can no longer reproduce because its reproductive organs have been surgically removed. In does, the ovaries, both cervixes, and the uterus are removed. This is called an ovariohysterovaginectomy, or spay. In bucks, the testicles and epididymis are removed. This is called castration.

In addition to the obvious advantage of preventing unwanted pregnancies and their associated risks (see "Raising Rabbits"), neutering offers your pet many health benefits. For example, because the reproductive organs are removed, they cannot become diseased with infections or cancer. The most common type of cancer in does is adenocarcinoma of the uterus. Depending on the breed, the incidence of uterine cancer in some does more than four years of age ranges from 50 to 80 percent. Uterine cancer can spread to other organs and is fatal. Spaying a doe can save her from developing cancer or infection of the ovaries and uterus. In bucks, castration prevents cancer and infections of the testicles and epididymis. If a rabbit has already developed disease of the reproductive organs,

surgical neutering may still be life saving if it is done in time.

The best time to neuter your rabbit is about six to twelve months of age, depending on breed and health status. Each animal's case must be considered individually to determine the best time to perform the procedure. Young, healthy animals often require less surgical and anesthesia time. Young females do not have as much abdominal fat as older females. Large amounts of fat in the abdominal cavity can make spay procedures more difficult. Young rabbits also tend to recover and heal faster than older ones. In addition, rabbits neutered early in life are less territorial, less likely to spray urine, and often have calmer dispositions.

Health Problems

The most common health problems seen in rabbits are gastrointestinal (GI) problems. Most GI problems are caused by feeding an incorrect diet. This means that the majority of rabbit illness can be prevented simply by feeding the right foods in the right amount. Clearly, what you feed your rabbit is one of the most important aspects of her health care (see "Feeding Your Rabbit").

Rabbits can suffer from noncontagious problems, such as trauma, obesity, heatstroke, and cancer. They may also suffer from contagious problems caused by bacteria, viruses, fungi, and parasites.

Your rabbit may not develop any of the problems listed below. If she does, though, you can use this valuable information to help your little companion. By detecting a health problem early, you can give your rabbit the care she needs right away to increase her chances of a speedy recovery.

If your rabbit has any of the medical conditions listed, contact your veterinarian for advice as soon as possible.

Rabbit diseases and disorders are described in great detail in many textbooks. This chapter discusses the more common problems most frequently encountered in pet rabbits and provides resources for readers to learn more details about specific health problems of special interest to them (see "Information").

Note that diseases and problems of the reproductive system may be prevented by neutering.

Anorexia

Anorexia is lack of appetite or refusal to eat. It is often the first sign your rabbit will give you that she has a problem, so watch her closely. Rabbits stop eating for many reasons, including incorrect diet, gastrointestinal disease, gastrointestinal obstruction, dental problems, pain, stress, infection, parasitism, or cancer. Rabbits cannot go without eating for very long without developing serious problems, such as hepatic lipidosis (fatty liver) or gastric stasis or ileus (reduced or no movement of stomach or intestines). A rabbit that does not eat will die within a few short days. If your rabbit has not eaten for 24 hours, ask your veterinarian to examine her right away.

Gastrointestinal Problems

Gastrointestinal (GI) tract problems are the most common health problems seen in pet rabbits. Most GI problems are caused by feeding the wrong kind of diet. This means that most rabbit health problems can be prevented by feeding your pet the right foods in the right proportions (see "Feeding Your Rabbit").

Causes of GI problems include but are not limited to the following:
• Feeding an unbalanced diet, especially diets low in fiber but high in sugar, fat, and protein
• Bacterial diseases and bacterial overgrowth in the gut, caused by eating an incorrect diet low in fiber
• Gastric stasis (wool block), caused by a low-fiber diet, stress, dehydration, and accumulation of ingested hair

- Obstruction (hairballs, foreign material, carpet fibers, bits of plastic, tumors, adhesions from abdominal surgeries)
- Parasites, such as pathologic protozoa, especially coccidia (twelve species of the genus *Eimeria*); coccidia are the most common GI parasite in rabbits
- Stress
- Viral diseases: *Coronavirus, Rotavirus, Calicivirus, Papillomavirus*
- Unsanitary housing conditions
- Cancer of the GI tract (rabbits can have various types of GI tumors)

Signs of GI problems include the following:
- Anorexia
- Constipation
- Dehydration
- Smaller and fewer fecal pellets than usual
- Diarrhea
- Enlarged or distended abdomen
- Lethargy, depression
- Abnormal stance, drooped head
- Pain
- Weight loss

Respiratory Problems

Respiratory disease is arguably the second most common cause of illness and death in rabbits, following gastrointestinal problems. Most cases of rabbit respiratory disease are caused by *Pasteurella multocida*. However, other microorganisms and environmental factors can add to the problem. A rabbit suffering from respiratory disease may have one or more of the following signs:
- Difficulty breathing, snuffling, sneezing, wheezing
- Initially a clear and then a white nasal discharge; as the disease progresses, the nasal

=== T I P ===

Important!
- Rabbits cannot survive long without eating and will die within a few days.
- Rabbits that do not eat can develop fatal hepatic lipidosis (fatty liver disease).
- Rabbits cannot vomit because anatomical features specific to rabbits prevent this ability (see "Rabbit Characteristics").
- Rabbits are obligate nose breathers and do not normally breathe from their mouths.
- It is normal for pregnant does to pull hair, especially from their dewlaps, to build nests.
- It is difficult to examine a rabbit's small mouth. Rabbits do not like to have their mouths touched. A thorough mouth examination is a job for your veterinarian. It requires special equipment and sedation or anesthesia.

discharge is yellow and purulent (pus) and may blow out of the nostrils when the rabbit sneezes
- Irritated, inflamed nasal passages (rhinitis) and sinuses (sinusitis)
- Yellow-gray matted nasal discharge visible on front feet from animal grooming her face with forepaws
- Conjunctivitis, tear duct infection, purulent discharge around eyes, excessive tearing, skin infection, and hair loss on face
- Infection of the middle ears (discharge exudate may be present at base of ear canal), head tilt

(torticollis), rabbit may be uncoordinated and unable to maintain her balance, nystagmus (rapid eye movement side to side, or up and down)

- Abscesses of the skin and/or internal organs
- Pneumonia and heart problems (pericarditis)
- Sepsis (bacterial spread throughout the blood system and body)

Skin Problems

Parasites are a common cause of skin problems. The ear mite, *Psoroptes cuniculi*, can also spread to the limbs, feet, and perineum of a weak or debilitated rabbit. The fur and mange mite, *Cheyletiella parasitovorax* (common in California), causes dandruff and coat thinning along the back of the neck, back, and rump.

Rabbits parasitized by fleas can develop skin allergies with itching, redness, and sores. Rabbits housed outdoors commonly suffer from fly larvae (*Cuterebra* species) and maggot infestations. These can cause serious health problems for infested rabbits. *Cuterebra* larvae are large and pupate under the rabbit's skin, usually under the neck or in the axillary (armpit) and inguinal (groin) areas. They form swollen bumps with visible air holes. Infested rabbits may become severely debilitated, suffer from bacterial infection, and die of toxic shock. Surgical removal and antibiotics are necessary to treat this serious problem. Other, smaller fly species can deposit hundreds of eggs in a rabbit's fur, usually around the perineal area. These develop into maggots (fly larvae) that invade and destroy body tissue. Maggots must be removed and the dead tissue cleared away. Antibiotics and supportive care are necessary to save the rabbit's life.

Causes: Skin problems are also caused by bacteria. The *Myxomatosis* virus, spread by insect vectors, can cause skin tumors and lesions. Fungal (ringworm) infections are caused by *Trichophyton mentagrophytes* and occasionally *Microsporum*.

Pododermatitis is a painful, ulcerative condition of the hind feet caused by trauma and pressure to the skin. Despite the lay term "sore hocks," the hocks are rarely affected.

Hard wire or rough floors, dirty caging, inadequate space, foot thumping, obesity, and thinly haired feet all contribute to the problem. Pododermatitis usually begins with an ulcer on the foot that later becomes infected, scabbed, and sometimes abscessed. Some rabbits may have a genetic predisposition for (are prone to) developing pododermatitis. Treatment is difficult and includes antibiotics, clean caging, solid cage flooring or a solid resting board, and clean foot bandages (if the rabbit will wear them).

Other causes: Poor nutrition, an unbalanced diet, stress, unsanitary housing, and allergies can all cause skin problems.

Signs of skin problems include the following:
- Dry, flaky skin
- Dandruff
- Loss of fur (alopecia)
- Crusty skin
- Sores
- Abscesses
- Skin tumors
- Skin may or may not itch, depending on the cause

Neurologic Problems

Many things can adversely affect the nervous system. These include trauma and injury, infection, toxins (from bacteria, plants, or chemicals), metabolic disorders, and parasites.

Vestibular Dysfunction

The vestibular system helps rabbits keep their balance. This system coordinates eye movement by sensing the position of the head and body in relation to space, movement, and gravity. Information from the vestibular system is processed in the brain.

Vestibular dysfunction is characterized by head tilt (usually to the affected side), also called wry neck or torticollis. It can be caused by infection with the protozoal parasite *Encephalitozoon cuniculi* (also known as *Nosema cuniculi*), which infects the central nervous system. More commonly, head tilt can be caused by bacteria. *Pasteurella multocida* affects/infects the middle ear and causes vestibular dysfunction.

Paralysis

A broken back is the most common cause of hind limb paralysis in rabbits. It is a common and serious injury. Rabbits have well-muscled, powerful hindquarters. When they are startled, jump, or try to escape restraint, they may twist and fracture their back, usually at the 9th thoracic or 6th to 7th lumbar vertebrae. Often the spinal cord is transected, leaving the animal permanently paralyzed in the hind limbs, with no control of her bladder or anal sphincter. In most cases, the animal must be euthanized.

Urogenital Problems

Diseases of the urinary tract include stones (calculi) in the bladder, urethra, ureters, or kidneys. Urinary incontinence, infections, and cancer can also occur.

Diet plays a big role in the kind of urine a rabbit produces. Diets high in calcium, such as those high in commercial pellets and low in grass hay and green vegetables, produce urine that appears thick and creamy and contains large amount of calcium "sand" and crystals. Small amounts of sand and crystals are normal in rabbit urine. When calcium intake is excessive, though, stones can form and obstruct the urinary tract. Bacterial infection adds to the problem. The condition is painful and life threatening. Stone removal requires anesthesia, surgery, and antibiotics in most cases.

Rabbits suffering from stones blocking the urinary tract have difficulty urinating. They may strain to urinate or have urine scalding of the perineum from dribbling urine intermittently. Blood may be present in the urine. Sometimes the rabbit is unable to urinate at all. Rabbits with this problem show signs of pain, including tooth grinding and a hunched position. They are anorexic, lethargic, and often dehydrated. They need immediate veterinary care to survive.

Rabbits can also develop a calcium-rich clay-like "sludge" that is difficult to pass and often results in pain, decreased appetite, and often bloody urine. This sludge is often best managed medically rather than surgically.

Kidney (Renal) Failure

Kidney failure is a serious, debilitating condition in which the kidneys fail to function properly and the animal eventually dies. There are many causes of kidney failure, including eating the wrong kind of diet, infections, toxins, and old age.

Heatstroke

Rabbits are sensitive to high temperatures. They should be protected from direct sunlight and heat sources. When you transport your rabbit, never leave her in the car. On a warm day, the car can heat up to 120°F (49°C) in a few minutes, even with the windows partially open.

If your rabbit is exposed to high temperatures, she will stretch out flat to try to dissipate heat. Her body temperature can rise above 105°F (40.5°C). She will rapidly become weak, depressed, and ataxic (lack coordination). She may have convulsions before she becomes comatose. Without immediate emergency treatment, your rabbit will die.

To lower your rabbit's body temperature safely, submerge her in cool (not cold) water. Support her head above water so she can breathe. Check her temperature every five minutes. Normal rectal temperature for a rabbit is 99.1 to 102.9°F (38.5 to 40°C). Be careful not to overcool your rabbit! When your pet has cooled down, dry her and take her to your veterinarian immediately for follow-up care. She will need to be hospitalized and monitored for several days. She will require fluid therapy and medication to prevent kidney failure, brain damage, respiratory infection, and other problems caused by heatstroke.

Medications

Veterinarians specializing in exotic and small animal medicine have compiled a list of medications that they consider safe for rabbits. To be safe, give your pet only medicines prescribed by your veterinarian and give no more than the prescribed dose.

Never give your rabbit any medicine prescribed for you or your other pets.

Emergency First Aid Kit

Have the following available in an emergency first aid kit. You don't want to be hunting through your home to find any of these items when an emergency occurs.

✔ Veterinarian's phone number
✔ Phone number of the nearest emergency pet hospital that treats rabbits
✔ Poison Control Hotline (see "Information")
✔ Mineral oil
✔ Eye rinse, artificial tears, sterile saline solution for eyes
✔ Gentle antiseptic solution
✔ Small, flat, baby nail trimmers
✔ Syringes (without needles): 1 mL, 3 mL, 6 mL, and 12 mL for feeding and medicating
✔ Scissors
✔ Tweezers or small forceps
✔ Magnifying glass
✔ Small flashlight or penlight
✔ Gauze
✔ Cotton-tipped swabs
✔ Thermometer (digital) to take rectal temperature
✔ Clean towels
✔ Disposable vinyl gloves

Zoonotic Diseases

Zoonotic diseases are diseases that can be shared between animals and humans. Many species of animals are carriers of diseases that do not make them ill but can make people very sick. Likewise, people can carry diseases to which humans are resistant but that make other animal species ill. Some disease organisms cause illness in both humans and animals.

Rabbits can potentially spread some diseases (bacterial, viral, fungal) to humans through contact, bites, or scratches. For example, although ringworm is not common in pet rabbits, the fungus that causes ringworm,

Trichophyton mentagrophytes, can also cause ringworm in humans.

Thorough hand washing after handling animals is an effective way to help prevent the spread of disease.

When Surgery Is Necessary

In some cases, surgery may be the only way to treat or save your rabbit. Fortunately for today's rabbits, we have developed safer anesthetics and improved surgical and dental techniques. We also have smaller equipment designed specifically for use in rabbits. These advances make it possible for veterinarians to perform life-saving procedures successfully when they are needed.

Your rabbit might need surgery to:
- Repair an injury or laceration
- Biopsy or remove a tumor
- Remove an intestinal obstruction
- Extract an abscessed tooth
- Perform a Cesarian section
- Remove the reproductive organs (neutering)

Unavoidable Problems

Some medical conditions cannot be predicted or prevented. These include problems associated with age-related disorders and cancer. If your rabbit has a medical problem that cannot be cured, you can still keep her comfortable, feed her well, and give her lots of love until it is time to say good-bye.

Good-bye, Good Friend

Even with the very best care, your rabbit will eventually develop signs of old age or illness. She will no longer be able to enjoy life as she did when she was healthy. This will be a difficult and sad time for you because your rabbit may be suffering and you will not be able to cure her. Eventually, you will wonder if it is time to euthanize your precious pet. When you come to that point, it is time to ask your veterinarian for help and guidance.

Euthanasia is ending an animal's life humanely, peacefully, and painlessly. Euthanasia is usually done by first giving the rabbit a sedative to make her unconscious. When she can no longer feel pain, an injection of a lethal drug is given that ends her life almost instantly.

Your veterinarian can answer any questions you may have. Your veterinarian can also help to find a pet cemetery, have your pet cremated, or have her necropsied.

During this emotional time, take good care of yourself, and take time to grieve. Take comfort in the knowledge that you gave your rabbit the best care possible throughout her life. Try to let happy memories of your beloved friend replace your sorrow.

Necropsy

Necropsy is the study of body tissues after an animal dies to learn more about the cause of death. Necropsies give us valuable information about health problems and often help us learn how to treat or cure the problem in other animals.

If your rabbit dies or if you must have her euthanized, you may want to think about having your pet necropsied. You and your veterinarian could learn more about your rabbit's condition and share the information with others. This knowledge may, in some way, be used to help other rabbits in the future.

Rabbit Health Chart

Contact your veterinarian right away if your rabbit has any of these health problems.

Health Problem	Signs
Abscesses	Abscesses are well-encapsulated, firm lumps filled with a thick white material (exudates). In rabbits, abscesses can develop in one to several days or may be slow growing. Skin abscesses typically appear nonpainful, but abscesses in other tissues may be painful.
Anorexia	Refusal to eat, lack of appetite.
Barbering and hair pulling	Patchy areas of hair loss on the head and back where hair has been plucked or pulled.
Bite wounds	Puncture wounds, lacerations, pain, redness, swelling, bleeding, infection, abscesses.
Broken bones, especially broken back or limbs	Inability to walk, hind limb paralysis, lack of bladder and anal sphincter control.
Cancer	Anorexia, weight loss, depression, lethargy, may be internal or external, may have visible masses or discharge.
Constipation	Straining to pass hard, dry, small fecal pellets; lethargy; lack of appetite.

Causes	Need to Know
Bacterial infections: Bite wounds, dental disease, tooth root abscess, foreign bodies, and trauma. Abscesses may contain more than one species of bacteria. The most common are *Pasteurella multocida, Pseudomonas aeruginosa, Staphylococcus aureus, Proteus, Bacteroides,* and *Enterococcus.*	Abscesses can form in almost any tissue or organ in rabbits. Jaw, dental, hock, bone, joint, and skin abscesses are common. Abscesses can even form behind a rabbit's eyes. Abscesses are difficult to treat and often recur. Surgical excision and antibiotics are necessary.
Gastrointestinal problems, dental problems, stress, pain, illness, injury, bacterial and viral diseases, parasites, cancer.	Rabbits that refuse to eat die within a few days. Hepatic lipidosis may develop. Do not wait more than 24 hours to seek veterinary help.
Dominant rabbits barber subordinates. Ones on low-fiber diets pull and ingest hair.	Pregnant does normally pull hair from their dewlaps, front legs, and sides to build nests.
Animal attacks.	Gently clean the wound with an antiseptic. Stop bleeding by applying pressure to the area with gauze for several minutes. Check for broken bones and muscle and nerve damage. Ask your veterinarian about antibiotics and pain medication. If your rabbit was bitten by a wild animal or unvaccinated pet, discuss the possible risk of rabies with your veterinarian.
Improper handling may lead to a broken back or limb. Rabbits that are startled and jump in their cages may also break their backs or limbs.	When startled or mishandled, rabbits may twist and fracture their backs. Often the spinal cord is damaged and the animal is permanently paralyzed.
Cancer has many causes and is common in rabbits, especially uterine adenocarcinoma.	Encourage eating and drinking. Discuss treatment options with your veterinarian.
Insufficient water; warm, dry environment; dehydration; internal parasites; gastrointestinal obstruction; gastric stasis; ileus.	Encourage drinking, correct the diet, treat for parasites, if needed, cat laxatives and lubricants may be helpful.

Health Problem	Signs
Dehydration	Lethargy, weakness, skin tenting, dull expression.
Dental problems	Lack of appetite, drooling, dropping pieces of food from mouth; bleeding from mouth; pain.
Diarrhea	Soft, mucous, or liquid feces; irritation and fecal material around anus and hind limbs; dehydration, poor appetite, weight loss, lethargy.
Ear problems	Shaking head, scratching head and ears, inflammation, thick crusting in ears, head tilt, loss of balance. Ear canals can become plugged with debris.
Enteritis (intestinal inflammation)	Soft or pasty fecal material, lethargy.
Enterotoxemia (release of bacterial toxins in the gut)	Watery, brown diarrhea, may contain blood and mucus.
Eye problems	Discharge, tearing, matted with discharge, eyes partially closed, intraocular diseases, cataracts, hypopyon, uveitis, lens rupture.

Causes	Need to Know
Exposure to hot, dry environment; not drinking enough; bacterial and viral infections; parasites, stress; heat stroke.	Encourage drinking. Your rabbit may need fluid therapy administered by your veterinarian.
Malocclusion, infection, tooth root abscesses, trauma.	Rabbits with malocclusion need their teeth trimmed regularly throughout life. Malocclusion can be an inherited trait. Affected animals should not be used for breeding.
Incorrect diet, internal parasites, bacterial infection, such as *Escherichia coli* (Colibacillosis) and *Clostridium piliforme* (Tyzzer's Disease) or viral infections (Coronavirus, Rotavirus, Calicivirus), stress, toxins from bacterial overgrowth in the gut.	Encourage drinking and feed correct diet. If diarrhea is persistent or severe, your pet will need hospitalization, fluid therapy, and prescription medications.
Parasites, ear mites (*Psoroptes cuniculi*), bacterial infection (*Pasteurella multocida*), injury.	Ear mites are tiny but can be seen with the naked eye or with a microscope. Coat affected parts of the ear with mineral oil to help kill the mites and sooth the ears until you can take your pet to the veterinarian for an exam and a prescription medicine to kill the mites. Wait until the mites have been eradicated before cleaning your rabbit's ears as they will be painful and bleed. Thoroughly clean housing and accessories to prevent re-infestation.
Insufficient fiber in the diet leads to a bacterial imbalance in the intestinal tract; pathogenic bacteria include *Escherichia coli*, Pseudomonas, Campylobacter, and Salmonella.	Mucoid enteritis is a common cause of death in young rabbits two to four months of age. It can be prevented by feeding a high-fiber/low-carbohydrate diet.
Clostridium spiroforme	Weanling kits (3 to 6 weeks of age) are most commonly affected. Mortality is high, with death in 1–2 days.
Disease, infection (*Pasteurella multocida, Encephalitozoon cuniculi*), injury, irritating substances, foreign body.	Injured eyes are often painful and sensitive to light. Gently rinse eyes with mild eye rinse. Prescription medication may be needed.

Health Problem	Signs
Gastric and intestinal obstructions	Lethargy, anorexia, pain, rapid deterioration leading to death.
Gastric stasis and ileus (decreased stomach and intestinal movement), known as hairballs, wool block, or trichobezoars	Stomach filled with ingested hair, poor appetite, fewer and smaller fecal pellets than normal, may be lethargic, may show signs of pain (tooth grinding).
Fatty liver disease (hepatic lipidosis)	Lethargy, weakness, lack of appetite, weight loss, death
Heatstroke	Hot, weak, unresponsive, comatose.
Infections	Signs vary and include lack of appetite, lethargy, weight loss, pain.
Injury	Pain, anorexia, lethargy, inability to move normally, bleeding, swelling.
Neurological problems	Head tilt, posterior paresis, paralysis, incoordination, inability to maintain a normal body position, convulsions, seizures.

Causes	Need to Know
Eating a wide variety of nondigestible objects, such as hair, plastic, string, carpet fibers, and other foreign objects; tumors may also cause GI obstruction.	This life-threatening, painful condition requires surgical removal of the foreign object.
Stress, low-fiber diet, high-carbohydrate diet, dehydration, and other health problems, plus the accumulation of large amounts of hair in the GI tract from self-grooming. Although hair is often found in the stomachs of rabbits, hair is rarely implicated in obstruction. Excessive amounts of hair may be an indication that the diet is too low in fiber. Low-fiber diets can lead to stasis problems.	A high-fiber diet can prevent gastric stasis by stimulating GI motility (movement). Fluid therapy (and antibiotics, if needed) is the treatment of choice. Hepatic lipidosis can quickly develop. Hospitalization may be necessary. Important: The mistaken belief that papaya extract protein-digesting enzymes (available from pet stores) may help dissolve hair and solve the problem does little more than delay the owner from bringing the rabbit to the veterinarian for actual and potentially life-saving treatment.
Insufficient food intake, refusal to eat.	Hepatic lipidosis can develop rapidly and lead to death if not treated right away.
Exposure to high temperature, insufficient ventilation.	To cool your rabbit, submerge her in cool (not cold) water until her body temperature is normal (99.1 to 102.9°F–38.5 to 40°C). Take her to your veterinarian immediately.
Bacteria, viruses, fungi, protozoa.	Isolate from other animals, wash hands after handling, consult veterinarian.
Numerous causes: broken back or broken limbs are often caused by incorrect handling or restraint, falls, trauma, animal attacks.	If your rabbit is unable to walk, carefully slide a thin board under her as a stretcher. Transport her to your veterinarian immediately.
Trauma (especially broken backs and nerve damage), viruses, bacteria, fungi, parasites, toxins (lead), dietary insufficiencies (magnesium), epilepsy, brain abscesses. Inner ear infection caused by *Pasteurella multocida*. The microsporidian parasite *Encephalitozoon cuniculi* causes severe neurological problems including head tilt in dwarf breeds.	*Encephalitozoon cuniculi* causes many nervous system problems, including paralysis. It is spread between rabbits by swallowing infective spores that are shed in the urine. It may also be spread from doe to kit through the placenta. There is no cure for the disease. Affected animals should be isolated from other rabbits.

Health Problem	Signs
Parasites (external)	Dry, flaky skin, crusty sores, hair loss, abscesses, allergies, may itch.
Parasites (internal)	Diarrhea with mucus or blood, weight loss, young animals more severely affected.
Respiratory problems	Difficulty breathing, snuffling (snuffles), wheezing, sneezing, rhinitis, sinusitis, purulent (pus) nasal discharge (can be present on forepaws from rubbing face), pneumonia, anorexia, lethargy, weight loss, may result in death.
Skin problems	Dry, flaky skin, dandruff, loss of fur, crusty skin, may itch, abscesses, bumps, tumors.
Slobbers	Moist dermatitis under the chin and neck.
Urine scalding	Moist dermatitis and irritated skin.
Urogenital disease	Blood or pus discharge visible at opening to urinary tract (urethra), or vaginal bleeding.

Causes	Need to Know
Mites, fleas, flies, fly larvae *Cuterebra*.	Parasite eradication includes clean housing and antiparasitic products.
Coccidia Eimeria infects the GI tract. *Eimeria stiedae* blocks the bile ducts to the gall bladder and causes liver problems.	Coccidia are a common cause of rabbit illness. Rabbits may also have worms, but these usually do not make rabbits sick.
Bacterial infections (primarily *Pasteurella multocida*, also *Bordetella*), *Mycoplasma*, viruses, and fungi. Respiratory problems are worsened by ammonia in the air (from rabbit urine) and exposure to cold and allergens.	Respiratory disease is a common cause of rabbit illness. Respiratory diseases caused by bacteria and viruses are spread through the air by direct contact, or by contact with contaminated objects. A high-protein diet creates large amounts of ammonia in rabbit urine and irritates the rabbit's respiratory system.
Parasites: ear mites (*Psoroptes cuniculi*), mange mites (*Cheyletiella parasitovorax*), fleas, flies, fly larvae (*Cuterebra*); bacteria; viruses (myxomatosis); rarely fungi (ringworm), *Trichophyton mentagrophytes*, occasionally Microsporum.	Skin problems caused by parasites are treated with prescription medication. Larval infestation is a serious problem that requires veterinary care and antibiotics. Feeding a balanced diet and reducing stress can help many skin problems.
Drooling due to dental disease, wet dewlaps from drinking out of bowls, combined with *Pseudomonas aeruginosa* infection.	*Pseudomonas* bacteria may turn the fur a greenish color. When the problem is corrected, the hair can dry, the skin heals, and the discoloration goes away.
Constant contact with urine due to urinary problems such as cystitis or incontinence.	Clip hair, keep rabbit clean and dry, and keep cage clean.
Bacterial infection, cancer, *Encephalitozoon cuniculi* infection, urinary incontinence, bladder stones, sludge (diet related).	Encourage eating and drinking, consult your veterinarian for specific treatment.

RAISING RABBITS

It's a giant leap from the joys of caring for a companion rabbit or two to the responsibilities and expenses of raising rabbits. Before you undertake this challenging and demanding hobby, make sure you have very good reasons for raising rabbits—and that you have the knowledge, time, finances, and facilities to do it right!

Reasons for Raising Rabbits

Rabbits are so cute and so much fun that at some point, you might consider raising them as a hobby. Raising rabbits requires hard work, dedication, knowledge, and good judgment. You must understand genetics and know which animals complement each other and which are the most likely to produce quality offspring. In addition, you must be prepared for the many emergency situations and medical conditions associated with pregnancy, lactation, and peri-natal (newborn) care. Raising rabbits can be fun. It can also be challenging and very costly.

Raising rabbits is a complicated science and an art that extends beyond the scope of this pet manual. Many excellent books are available that delve into rabbit raising in great detail (see "Information"). This chapter will give you valuable information about rabbit reproduction to help you decide whether raising rabbits is the right hobby for you.

Why do you want to raise rabbits? Historically, people have raised rabbits for many reasons: companionship, exhibition, food, and fur (pelts). (The latter two categories will not be discussed in this book and are usually done on a large, industrial scale for profit.) Raising rabbits to produce quality pets and to compete in rabbit shows can be a very rewarding hobby. However, you must consider why you want to raise rabbits before hopping into such a big endeavor. If your reasons are profit oriented, please reconsider. Raising rabbits is an expensive hobby when you add up the costs of purchasing quality breeding stock, housing, necessary materials and supplies, food, and providing health care. In addition, dealing with the inevitable loss of animal lives due to reproductive problems and bunny mortality is heartbreaking. For example, does can suffer and die of pregnancy-related complications. In less than ideal conditions, bunny mortality can be high. Rabbits may have genetic problems that can affect their health and be passed on to their offspring.

When you raise rabbits, you must find good homes for each one of them or keep the animals yourself. There is a surplus of rabbits in need of good homes. So before you breed your rabbits, make sure you have homes for them and that you are not adding to the pet rabbit overpopulation problem. Don't forget that you will have to also keep or find homes for your retired breeders as well as your bunnies.

If you want to raise rabbits because rabbits are your passion and your goals are to produce healthy, well-socialized, attractive pets, improve breeding stock, reduce the incidence of inherited health problems, and educate people about these wonderful animals (and you want to be a responsible, ethical breeder) then you have your work cut out for you!

To-Do List for the New Rabbit Breeder

1. Make sure there is a market for pet rabbits in your area and that you will be able to find homes for all of your bunnies.

2. Learn as much as possible about rabbits and rabbit reproduction.

3. Study the American Rabbit Breeders Association *Standard of Perfection* for the breed of your choice.

4. Write your health guarantees, contracts, sales policies, and information pamphlets. Include a written policy saying that you will take back rabbits that you sell that do not work out for the buyers or will help the buyers find new homes for the rabbits if they cannot keep the rabbits for any reason.

5. Choose a veterinarian.

6. Join a rabbit club and attend both educational seminars and rabbit shows.

7. Visit rabbit breeders and rabbitries. Carefully select your breeding stock. Ask an experienced rabbit breeder to be your mentor.

8. Identify (by tattoo or microchip) your rabbits.

9. When your rabbits are at least six months of age, register them with the American Rabbit Breeders Association (see "Information").

10. Keep detailed breeding records and accurate pedigrees.

11. Learn about the genetics of your chosen breed(s).

Remember
Responsible breeders always make sure they have loving homes lined up for their bunnies before they breed their animals.

Rabbit Reproduction

Sexual maturity (puberty)	Depends on breed, ranges from 4 to 12 months, dwarf and small breeds reach puberty earlier than large and giant breeds. Bucks mature slower than does, about one month later.
Recommended breeding age	Depends on breed, guidelines only: Bucks 6 to 10 months Does 4 to 10 months
Estrus	Rabbits are induced ovulators. Copulation triggers ovulation, which occurs approximately 10 hours after mating.
False pregnancy	Induced by sterile copulation and lasts 16 days.
Gestation (pregnancy)	30 to 35 days. The rabbit uterus consists of two completely separate uterine horns and two cervixes, so embryos do not migrate between horns as in many other species.
Placentation	Hemochorial: Allows close contact between maternal and fetal circulation, similar to humans.
Implantation	Approximately 7 days after mating.
Nest building	Does pull hair from their dewlaps, front legs, and underside to build a nest for their bunnies.
Litter size	Varies, on average 4 to 10 bunnies (also called kits or kittens).
Lactation	Does have 8 to 10 teats. They visit their bunnies once daily, in the early morning, for about 5 minutes to feed them. Rabbit milk is high in fat and protein content (13.1 percent fat, 12.3 percent protein, 1.9 percent lactose). It may take some time for a doe's milk to come down, and some does may not feed bunnies during the first 24 hours or more. In this case, bunnies must be supplemented until the doe can feed them.
Weaning	3 to 6 weeks of age: Bunnies should not be weaned until they are at least one month old.
Recommended time to use for breeding	Depending on animal's health and breed, 1 to 3 years. Rabbits should be retired from breeding after they reach 3 years of age.
Duration of fertility	Approximately 6 years.
Lifespan	Approximately 9 years.

12. Have an emergency preparedness plan in place, including a method for animal evacuation in case of disaster (flood, fire, earthquake, hurricanes) and a cooling and ventilation system in place for the rabbits in case of heat waves.

13. Purchase a generator for back-up power in case of power failures so you can maintain your breeding colony at comfortable temperatures, ventilation, and lighting.

14. Consider how many animals you have time, money, and space to keep. Keep animal numbers reasonable so you can give each rabbit the excellent care it deserves.

15. Make sure you have homes reserved for your bunnies before you breed your rabbits.

16. Have a plan for your retired breeders. Rabbits can't spend their entire lives reproducing. At some point, they must "retire." Can you keep them, or do you have loving homes lined up for them?

As a rabbit breeder, you will have active breeders, retired breeders, show animals, pet animals, and several babies and young adolescent animals that you will retain to keep your hobby hopping. Are you prepared and able to manage these challenges and responsibilities?

Rabbit Reproduction

Rabbits are notoriously prolific breeders. A classic example is the case of a single pair of rabbits introduced into Victoria, Australia, in 1859. Thirty-one years later, the rabbit population had exploded to more than 20 million. In commercial industries, rabbits produce a litter every 2 to 4 months and up to 7 to 11 litters until they are retired. In the wild, a doe can produce 15 to 45 offspring in a year. The rabbit's amazing reproductive abilities have allowed this species to survive for millions of years despite severe predation.

Breeding Behavior

When does are receptive to breeding, they are sometimes restless. They will rub their chins on their cage and surroundings. Receptive does have a slightly swollen, purplish vulva. Does are receptive to breeding about 72 hours after kindling (giving birth). Does are remarkable in their ability to produce four to five litters per year. They produce five litters annually if they are bred 42 days after kindling, averaging one litter every 74 days. They produce four litters annually if they are bred 56 days after kindling.

Does should be taken to the buck's cage for breeding because they are very territorial and might become aggressive and injure the buck. The buck may circle the doe. If she is receptive, she will raise her hindquarters (lordosis). Copulation usually takes place rapidly, within a few minutes. When copulation is completed, the buck will squeal and fall over onto his side. This is normal breeding behavior. The female can be immediately removed and returned to her cage.

Does can be palpated to detect pregnancy as early as 9 days after mating. Your veterinarian can show you how to palpate your doe gently without injuring the embryos.

Sexing the Bunnies

Hold the bunny firmly around the shoulders with one hand. Rest the bunny on its back,

with its rump in the palm of your other hand, grasping the tail between your index and middle fingers. Place your thumb above the genital area, and apply a light pressure. If the bunny is a buck, the penis will protrude slightly. If it is a doe, a slit will be present.

Supplemental Feeding

Weigh your bunnies at least once weekly. If their mother does not have milk or if they are thin or not gaining weight, they will need to be supplemented.

If your bunnies need supplemental feeding, use the following guidelines.

Birth to 2 weeks: Esbilac can be used to substitute for rabbit's milk. Ask your veterinarian to show you how to feed liquid to your bunny and how much to feed. Feed once every 24 hours. Does normally feed their bunnies in the early morning, so this is a good time to supplement the bunnies. Use a moistened cotton ball to massage the bunny's genital area very gently to stimulate urination and defecation.

Age 2 to 4 weeks: Esbilac, alfalfa hay, pellets, and greens (wash well to remove contaminants and pesticides!). Introduce new foods gradually. Use a moistened cotton ball to massage the bunny's genital area very gently to stimulate urination and defecation.

Age 4 to 8 weeks: Use the same diet as previously plus gradually introduce fresh vegetables.

Bunny Progress	
Birth	1 to 2.5 ounces (30 to 80 g)
10 days of age	Eyes open
3 weeks of age	Bunnies start exploring outside of nest, weaning begins
6 to 8 weeks of age	Bunnies are weaned and leave home

THE RABBIT CONNOISSEUR

As a rabbit enthusiast, you know there is no limit to the fun you can have with your rabbit. Now is a great time to take the next leap and participate in rabbit events, shows, exhibitions, clubs, and educational seminars.

Breeds, Colors, Clubs, and Shows

Just like people, every rabbit differs in personality and appearance. Rabbits come in a variety of sizes, colors, coat textures, ear lengths, and ear carriage. The American Rabbit Breeders Association (ARBA) currently recognizes 47 breeds. The ARBA publications describe each breed and its history in detail and provide charts with color photographs suitable for framing (see "Information").

Genetic inheritance of coat and eye color, body conformation, coat texture, ear length, and ear carriage are all very complicated topics. In any breeding program, the rabbit's health, temperament, and conformation are the most important factors.

Your bunny is a beloved family companion. If you think she is gorgeous enough to compete against the very best, give her a chance! Check the ARBA website for show information and locations. You'll have a lot of fun, you'll learn a lot, and you'll make new friends, too. So make some room on that shelf—it just might be your bunny's turn to bring home the blue ribbon!

Activities

If your rabbit is outgoing, adventurous, or social, she may enjoy other activities in addition to going to rabbit shows, riding in her bunny stroller, or walking on a leash in the park with you. She may make a wonderful pet therapy bunny, visiting and bringing happiness to people in nursing homes. She may be a great ambassador for her species by visiting school classrooms and helping educate children about rabbits and responsible pet care. Many rabbit clubs organize fun activities for rabbits. For example, the San Diego House Rabbit Society holds events such as Bunnyfest to help rabbits in need and to educate the public about rabbits. Bunnyfest is a fun event, complete with educational materials,

French Angora

lunch, rabbit supplies of all kinds, and contests, games, and activities for rabbit lovers and their beloved bunnies.

Enraptured with Rabbits

Rabbits are delightful, affectionate pets. They have brought friendship, companionship, entertainment, and happiness to many thousands of people. From the Iberian Peninsula to medieval warrens to worldwide expansion and finally into loving homes, the rabbit is a world traveler. The bright-eyed, beautiful bunny is an endearing animal that deserves her status today as one of the most popular pets in the world.

So the next time you cuddle with your rabbit and look into her big, bright eyes and find yourself helplessly smitten, remember that thousands of rabbit fans share your enthusiasm and are as enraptured with rabbits as you are. You're in good company!

Rabbit Breeds

**Small Breeds
(2 to 6 pounds/
1 to 2.7 kg)**
American Fuzzy Lop
Britannia Petite
Dutch
Dwarf Hotot
Florida White
Havana
Himalayan
Holland Lop
Jersey Wooly
Mini Lop
Mini Rex
Netherland Dwarf
Polish
Silver
Tan

**Large Breeds
(9 to 11 pounds/
4 to 5 kg)**
American
American Chinchilla
Beveren
Californian
Champagne
d'Argent
Cinnamon
Creme d'Argent
English Lop
Giant Angora
Hotot
New Zealand
Palomino
Satin
Silver Fox

**Medium Breeds
(6 to 9 pounds/
2.7 to 4 kg)**
American Sable
Belgian Hare
English Angora
English Spot
French Angora
Harlequin
Lilac
Rex
Rhinelander
Satin Angora
Silver Marten
Standard Chinchilla

**Giant Breeds
(11 pounds and
over/
5 kg and over)**
Checkered Giant
Flemish Giant
French Lop
Giant Chinchilla

INFORMATION

Organizations

American Rabbit Breeders Association
P.O. Box 5667
Bloomington, IL 61702
(309) 664-7500
www.arba.net
E-mail: info@arba.net

American Veterinary Medical Association
1931 N. Meacham Road, Suite 100
Schaumburg, IL 60173-4360
(847) 925-8070
www.avma.org
E-mail: avmainfo@avma.org

Association of Exotic Mammal Veterinarians
P.O. Box 396
Weare, NH 03281-0396
www.aemv.org
E-mail: info@aemv.org

United States Department of Agriculture
Animal and Plant Health Inspection Services
www.aphis.usda.gov

Magazines

Critters USA
Annual Guide to Caring for Exotic Mammals
Irvine, CA: Fancy Publications
(949) 855-8822
www.animalnetwork.com

Journal of Exotic Pet Medicine
New York, NY: Elsevier Saunders
www.exoticpetmedicine.com

Rabbits USA
Irvine, CA: Fancy Publications
(949) 855-8822
www.animalnetwork.com

Books

American Rabbit Breeders Association, Inc. *Raising Better Rabbits and Cavies. Official Guide Book.* Bloomington, IL: American Rabbit Breeders Association, Inc., 2011.

American Rabbit Breeders Association, Inc. *The Rabbit and Cavy Project.* Bloomington, IL: American Rabbit Breeders Association, Inc., 2011.

American Rabbit Breeders Association, Inc. *Standard of Perfection.* Bloomington, IL: American Rabbit Breeders Association, Inc., 2011.

Johnson-Delaney, Cathy. *Exotic Companion Medicine Handbook.* Lake Worth, FL: Wingers Publishing, 1996.

Harriman, M. *House Rabbit Handbook. How to Live with an Urban Rabbit.* Alameda, CA: Droollery Press, 2005.

Nowak, Ronald, ed. *Walker's Mammals of the World.* Baltimore and London: The Johns Hopkins University Press, 1999.

Quessenberry, K. E., and E. V. Hillyer. *Ferrets, Rabbits, and Rodents. Clinical Medicine and Surgery.* New York, NY: W. B. Saunders, 2003.

Verhoef-Verhallen, E. *The Complete Encyclopedia of Rabbits and Rodents.* Groningen, the Netherlands: Rebo Publishers, 1997.

Weisbroth, S. H., R. E. Flatt, and A. L. Kraus. *The Biology of the Laboratory Rabbit.* New York, NY: Academic Press, Inc.,1974.

Whitman, B. D. *Domestic Rabbits and Their Histories. Breeds of the World.* Overland Park, KS: Leathers Publishing, 2004.

I N D E X

About the Author

Sharon Vanderlip, DVM, has a Bachelor of Science degree in zoology from the University of California at Davis and a degree in veterinary medicine. Dr. Vanderlip has provided veterinary care to exotic, wild, and domestic animals for more than 30 years. She has published in scientific journals and has authored more than 20 books on pet care. Dr. Vanderlip owns a specialty practice, has served as clinical veterinarian for the University of California at San Diego School of Medicine, has collaborated on research projects with the San Diego Zoo, and is former chief of veterinary services for the National Aeronautics and Space Administration. Dr. Vanderlip owned, raised, and exhibited Satin rabbits for years and has cared for hundreds of rabbits in practice. She may be contacted for seminars at *www.sharonvanderlip.com.*

Acknowledgments

A *huge* thank you to my husband, Jack Vanderlip, DVM, for sharing his expertise in exotic and laboratory animal medicine, for his critical review of the final manuscript, and for taking care of everything at home and in the practice so that I could have time to research and write this book. Without his help, this book would have never been completed! Thanks to our daughter, Jacquelynn, for her enthusiasm and for providing photos for the book. Special thanks to San Diego County 4-H members for providing many rabbits to photograph. Finally, thank you to my editor, Anthony Regolino, for his kind help and consideration.

Cover Credits

Jacquelynn Holly: front cover, back cover; Shutterstock: inside front cover, inside back cover.

Photo Credits

Jacquelynn Holly: pages 4, 5, 7, 8, 9, 12, 13 (top and bottom), 15, 16 (top and bottom), 18 (top), 31, 51, 90, 91; Shutterstock: pages 2, 19, 20, 22, 25, 29, 30, 32, 33, 40, 45, 46, 50, 53, 59, 60, 69, 84, 86, 89; Sharon Vanderlip: pages 6, 10, 17, 18 (bottom), 21, 34, 36, 37, 38, 42, 43, 48, 49, 56, 57, 58, 63, 64, 65, 66, 70, 85, 92.

© Copyright 2012 by Barron's Educational Series, Inc.

All inquiries should be addressed to:
Barron's Educational Series, Inc.
250 Wireless Boulevard
Hauppauge, NY 11788
www.barronseduc.com

ISBN: 978-1-4380-0092-3

Library of Congress Control Number: 2012001689

Library of Congress Cataloging-in-Publication Data
Vanderlip, Sharon Lynn.
    Rabbits / Sharon Vanderlip.
        p. cm. — (Complete pet owner's manual)
    Includes index.
    ISBN: 978-1-4380-0092-3 (pbk.)
    1. Rabbits. I. Title.
    SF453.V36 2012
    636.932'2—dc 23   2012001689

Printed in China
9 8 7 6 5 4 3 2 1